Collecting
Shelley Pottery

Robert Prescott-Walker

Francis Joseph
ISBN 1-870703-67-7

Acknowledgements

As usual, my thanks go to various people without whom this book would not have been possible. Indeed come to think of it, I could even go back as far as my ceramics tutor, Gordon Elliott, who nurtured my interest in ceramics as well as having to put up with my hand-written essays, before it become necessary for me to purchase a typewriter. These were in the days when computers were not quite so readily available.

I am particularly grateful to Alexander Clement and Julie Mckeown, indeed to Royal Doulton (UK) Ltd, for allowing me access to the Shelley Archive and for putting up with me during my research.

Grateful thanks also to Sharon Ashbolt (Sotheby's, Sussex) for extricating and sending illustrations which proved to be very helpful, also to Christina Donaldson (now Prescott-Walker) (formerly Sotheby's, London) for gathering even more illustrations. I am also very grateful to Sotheby's (UK) for allowing me to use the above mentioned illustrations.

I would very much like to thank the two former Shelley pottery employees for sharing their professional experiences and working knowledge of the firm, together with the illuminative talks I had with Donald Brindley, former art director of the E. Brain & Co. Ltd, Foley Bone China pottery.

I am also very grateful to Nick Jones and Jeff Peak of Alfies Antiques, London and to Beverley and Beth of Church Street, London for supplying almost all of the items used to illustrate this book and their patience during the photography.

Not to be forgotten is the Shelley Group who kept me informed for a number of years about various issues and aspects of the pottery. The open dissemination and discussion which is the policy of the group has been of great benefit over the years.

© 1999 Francis Joseph Publications

ISBN 1-870703-67-7

Published by Francis Joseph,
5 Southbrook Mews, London SE12 8LG

Photography: Trevor Leek

Typesetting by E J Folkard Print Services, 199 Station Road, Crayford, Kent DA1 3QF

Printed by Greenwich Press Ltd, Eastmoor Street, London SE7 8LX

Front cover photograph: Cottage – 2 pattern, designed in 1928 by Eric Slater

Contents

Introduction

I should just like to point out that what I have endeavoured to cover within these pages is a broad outlook of what has become known as the Shelley Pottery, although should perhaps be more correctly called the Wileman & Co. Foley Pottery and subsequent Shelley Pottery. This book is aimed at the person who wishes to start collecting Shelley or as been building up a collection but needs some guidance. Hopefully there will also be something of interest for those 'official', long-time, hardened collectors. At this point I should perhaps rather shamefully admit that I am a lapsed ex-member of the Shelley Group (UK) of some years standing. Yes, that really is me peering out from the pages of the number 7 issue of the Newsletter, back in March 1988.

If there is one thing that I hope readers of this book will develop more than anything else it is the confidence to pick up and handle the objects of their desire and thereby learn a great deal more about the objects than just reading about them in books. Over the years I have learnt, and I'm sure most other collectors will say the same, that your senses are your best learning tools; once practised and trained in the art of looking at and handling the wares, they will be your greatest asset.

I hope also that the reader will gain a better overall knowledge of how the Shelley Pottery fits into the wider scheme of things, how it developed compared to its contemporaries and rivals, how it set out to achieve its aims and why it was such an important pottery. When compared to so many other products of the Potteries of a comparable period, Shelley wares are like a breath of fresh air. Just a quick glance at a collection of the designs reveals a light, airy and uncluttered aspect, even at times humorous, and not just the nursery wares. There really is an elegance, style, craftsmanship and quality about the finished product that has stood the test of time.

Shelley China, formerly Wileman & Co. had two highly successful periods in terms of production. This success, however, was for the most part the product of exemplary business management and consumer awareness, not to mention a versatility and knowledge that could be turned to invention. By looking in more detail at some of the issues and daily concerns that went on behind the scenes at the Foley China Works, the successes and failures of the company become more apparent. One thing particularly noticeable is that as a business the Foley China Works was, in the main, a model of how to run a successful business. At the same time, it was largely the reputation that they had worked so hard to develop and maintain throughout the Twentieth century, that was to ultimately lead to the firm's demise. Unfortunately, as we shall see, just when the new 'Avon' shape and new pattern designs, such as 'Apollo' and 'Aegean', were being launched, reflecting the typically innovative and original work associated with the pottery, the rug was pulled from under their feet.

The Shelley pottery business was one of high volume turnover of reasonably priced wares (for bone china that is) with the decorative and visual appearance of more expensive wares. There was no room for vast quantities of waste or for too much consideration in regard to the refinement of the body. Shelley were not trying to be another top flight Wedgwood, Minton or Spode, each with their own high standards and quality controls which saw vast quantities of ware being smashed as substandard; they were after a different place in the market. In the initial years of establishing the business it was more important to have some sort of recovery for as much of every kiln firing as possible. In other words there is a good reason why there are different categories or standards of ware produced by the pottery, with certain patterns and shapes only appearing under certain categories; namely cost effectiveness.

In the later years the dependence on the export market, seemingly at the cost of building up the home market, together with diversification away from the wares lead to merger with the Allied English Potteries company, ultimately the end of the name Shelley.

For the collector however, all is far from lost, although it is interesting to note that the early bone china tea wares produced in the 1880s and 1890s seem to be making a comeback on the collecting scene, as do the Harmony ware ranges. Quite frankly, I do not feel I even need to mention the continuing popularity of Dainty White, in all it's variations, as it is and always has been tremendously well known and popular. Just to throw down a challenge, you tell me just how and why Dainty White is so popular, why do you collect or want to collect it and what does it mean to you?

There are pieces of earthenware known to have been made by a Michael Shelley, a mug dating from the 1780s, who was the first potter involved with the Gladstone Pottery, Longton, Stoke-on-Trent, as well a plaque dated 1799 by a John Shelley. For our purposes however the Shelley story begins in 1853 at the site of the Foley Potteries.

Chronology

1827 John Smith built a group of potteries later to become known as the 'Foley Potteries'. Factory let to Thomas & George Elkin, John King Knight and a John Bridgewood.

1833 Thomas Elkin withdrew from partnership.

1840 John Bridgewood retired.

1847 George Elkin retired.

1853 John King Knight having continued alone from 1847, brought in Henry Wileman as a partner.

1856 Knight retires leaving Henry Wileman in charge.

1860 Henry Wileman builds the 'Foley China Works'.

1864 Henry Wileman dies leaving his two sons, Charles & James, J. & C. Wileman, in charge.

1866 Partnership broke down. Charles took on the 'Foley China Works' and James the earthenware side, 'The Foley Potteries'.

1870 Charles retires and James gains control of both works.

1872 Joseph Ball Shelley joins James Wileman in partnership of the china works side of the business. Trading as 'Wileman & Co.'.

1881 Percy Shelley, Joseph's son, joins the firm, 'Wileman & Co.'.

1884 James retires from the china works, leaving Joseph and Percy in charge.

1892 James retires, closing the original earthenware works. These buildings were let on and off until 1984 when they were demolished.

1894 New earthenware works built next to the 'Foley China Works'.

1896 Joseph Shelley dies. Percy Shelley sole proprietor.
Frederick Rhead appointed Art Director
Rowland Morris sold designs to Percy Shelley

1905 Walter Slater becomes Art Director

1910 Percy Shelley adopted the trademark Shelley China.

1913 Percy Shelley's sons, Percy Norman and Vincent Bob joined the firm.

1919 Kenneth Jack joined the firm having graduated from Birmingham University after the war. Eric Slater, son of Walter, joins the firm.

1925 The name of 'Shelleys' was finally registered as the company trade name. Hilda Cowham employed as a designer for nursery wares.

1926 Mabel Lucie Attwell engaged to add further designs to the nursery wares.

1929 The Shelley Potteries becomes a limited company.

1932 Percy Shelley retires, moving to Bournemouth.

1933 Jack Shelley suddenly dies in hospital while recuperating from an operation.

1937 Percy Shelley dies after a long illness. Walter Slater retires as Art Director to be succeeded by his son, Eric. Walter dies a year later.

1945 Vincent Bob Shelley dies (29th December) leaving Percy Norman, his elder brother as sole director.

1946 A month after Vincent Bob's death, Eric Slater and Ralph Tatton were elected to the board of Directors. Later in the year Vincent Bob's son Alan joins the firm as the sales director, to be joined by his brother, Donald, two years later after graduating from Cambridge University. The fourth and final generation had joined the firm. Earthenware works closes.

1956 Shelley Electric Furnaces Ltd. established in May by Donald Shelley

1965 Shelley Potteries renamed Shelley China Limited.

1966 Norman Shelley dies (May). The Shelley family's long association with the firm, now known as Shelley China Limited, ends with the take over by Allied English Potteries. The works was renamed the Montrose Works and the production of Royal Albert ware was transferred there.

1971 Doulton Group took over the works and the name of Shelley was the name alive by registering "no returns" every year at Companies House. Therefore, should they wish to do so new wares could be marketed using the Shelley name. Today only a few of the original buildings remain and they are now being used to house the Sir Henry Doulton School of Sculpture.

The Early Years

As with many businesses, it took time for a ceramic manufacturer to establish a niche in such a competitive and concentrated market as Stoke-on-Trent. In this case the early years take us back to 1853 when Henry Wileman was first associated with the Foley pottery, joining Mr. J.K. Knight as a partner. Only three years later Henry Wileman was able to call the business his own following the retirement of Mr. Knight.

What is now known as the Foley China Works, the home of the Wileman and later Shelley Pottery, was part of a complex of buildings erected in 1827 by John Smith, whose family owned large areas of Fenton. The pottery was in fact one of several potteries using the name of Foley.

Wileman & Co. until the 1870s seems to have been a rather uneventful pottery, producing rather sub-standard china and earthenware of a fairly plain nature. Indeed until about 1870 there does not seem to have been a trademark, certainly not a registered one, in use on the wares. In 1864 Charles and James took over the business following the death of their father Henry Wileman, although two years later the brothers decided to split the business, James taking on the earthenware side, 'The Foley Potteries', while Charles was responsible for the china works, The Foley China Works'. Shortly after James took over both sides of the business following the retirement of his brother.

It should be remembered that during this period there were a number of economic, aesthetic and political factors that were colouring the products of the British pottery industry. The 1860s saw the re-emergence of Japanese design, most significantly and visibly at the 1862 International Exhibition and then at the Paris Exhibition of 1867, and at the 1876 Philadelphia Centennial Exhibition. As a consequence the 'Oriental' style, or rather loose versions of it, proliferated on the surfaces of much domestic, fancy and even 'artistic' ceramic products for many years to come both across Europe and in America.

This was also a period of rapid industrial expansion and growth; mass-production and mechanisation making available to the ever increasingly moneyed middle class wares to furnish the house, gadgets to help clean or help in the kitchen, as well as many other general goods. Rapidly improving communication and transport started to break down the barriers between countries, creating a healthy market for exported goods and general free trade. This led to a greater diversity of choice for the consumer.

Export markets were to prove of vital importance to the development of the Wileman Pottery. James Wileman was very aware of the importance of making wares that were suitable for markets other than those of home. The opening up of world markets and the advent of rapidly developing and competitive pottery business in various parts of the world meant that British manufacturers no longer had the luxury of the monopolies they once had. Perhaps to facilitate this change James took on a new partner Joseph Ball Shelley in 1872, partner that is in the china works and not the earthenware business. It was during this period that numerous advertisements are found in the trade journals extolling the virtues of having established a 'Home and Foreign trade', naming places such as 'France, Spain, the Levant, East, West and South Africa, the Straits Settlements,' etc. in these advertisements.

Some years later, following a visit by Percy to the 1893 Chicago Exhibition, many new designs were developed specifically for sale in North America and Canada, with Shelleys establishing links with agents in the USA and Canada, as well as in Melbourne, Australia.

With the rejuvenated firm making great strides, James Wileman retired in 1884, which

Sgraffito ware teapot and jug. Taken from the Art Journal magazine 1905.

allowed Joseph Shelley and his son Percy, who had joined the firm in 1881 having graduated from London University, to see through the final stages of development that would transfer the pottery into a highly prosperous and acknowledged name. The Pottery finally came into its own on the death of Joseph Shelley in 1896, during which period Percy Shelley was able to take complete control of the firm, employing the skills of various designers, including the highly reputed painter of fish, game and landscapes, F. Micklewright, and the ceramic modeller Rowland Morris. It was Morris who was to design the most long lasting and familiar of all the Shelley shapes, 'Dainty White'. Registered in 1896, only two years before Morris's death, the Dainty shape outlasted the demise of the pottery in 1966, Allied English Potteries having to fulfil orders after the take-over. Produced in a more refined body than previous Wileman wares, Dainty White appealed to a vast audience in Britain but was even more enthusiastically taken up in America, Australia and South Africa, to name but a few. Although clothed in endless patterns throughout its long history, defying the ebb and flow of the various fashion and tastes throughout the twentieth century, it was in it's most simple plain white and white and gilt form that Dainty, and it's variations, had its widest appeal. Today the Dainty shape in all its variations is keenly sought after throughout the world, in fact, such is the popularity, history and variety of the Dainty shape, it could quite happily fill the pages of a book by itself.

Perhaps the most notable designer to be employed by the factory was the young and talented craftsman Frederick Rhead. Frederick was from a distinguished Potteries family, many of whom, had made, and would continue to make, significant contributions to the potters art, both in Britain and perhaps even more significantly, in America. It was Frederick's daughter, Charlotte, who produced such individual and highly artistic designs for the A .G. Richardson works and subsequently as art director for Wood & Son, Burslem. Frederick Hurten Rhead, Charlotte's brother, having been art director at Thomas Forester & Sons, moved to America in 1902 where he was to have a major impact on the development of artistic pottery. There he introduced a wealth of decorative techniques and skills, over a period of forty years, that formed the bedrock of much American art and studio pottery to come.

The period that Frederick Rhead was working for Wileman, from 1896 to 1905, coincides, more or less, with what might be termed the 'experimentalist' period, dating from the early 1870s through to about 1910. This 'experimentalist' period, certainly in terms of the ceramics industry, saw huge strides taken in the development and production of a vast array of wares in the pursuit of commercialism, as well as the ideology as expressed by William Morris. Such growth and experimentation developed on the back of an increasing technical knowledge of materials, amongst other things, as well as the growing availability of new sources of raw materials from various parts of the world.

Spano-Lustra Lobster vase and an Urbato vase. Taken from the Art Journal magazine 1905.

The rapid development in communications and opening up of International borders meant that information and knowledge of artistic matters beyond British shores was soon very accessible. Exhibitions of newly acquired objects from foreign shores, mostly belonging to private collectors and museums, were put on display and often traveled around the country. From such collections artists, designers, critics and the general public were able to draw inspiration and knowledge, increasing their design vocabulary.

Just to indicate some of the interest seen in the ranges produced by F Rhead, we need only look to the brightly coloured polychrome architectural panels of the Italian Della Robbia family as well as to Perisan, Hispano-Moresque and Rhodian ceramic wares, exhibited and written about during the 1880s and 1890s. Not only did these wares inspire the bold use of blocks of colour and decorative style, but also many of the shapes that were used. There is often a strong Japanese influence, as seen in the use of botanical designs and cranes in flight, as well as in the more fluent and swirling botanical studies, also reflected in some of the shapes. The interest, generated through William Morris, in the revival of medieval styles can also be seen in the work of Rhead, while his Faience wares reflect more fully an Arts and Crafts inspiration. Such inspiration is visible in many of Rhead's designs including utilitarian wares, vases, jugs, basins and bowls, etc. In fact, one of the greatest virtues of Rhead's designs is their diversity, not to mention humour.

Rhead's humorous side can be seen in the production of numerous jugs and ornaments that were pure flights of fantasy, in a similar vein to the Martin Brothers models, and appropriately named 'grotesques'. Bernard Moore was also to make such animals which, like those of Rhead, seem to be based on imported Japanese and Chinese models. At about the same time Rhead also produced a series of whimsical Intarsio ware teapots based on political and other related figures. One such teapot known as 'Votes for Women' and appropriately modelled with a female figure now commands between £2000-£3000/$3900-$6150, being particular rare compared to others in the series.

The importance of the contribution made by Rhead to the Wileman Pottery has largely been over looked, certainly underplayed, his name normally being associated with the

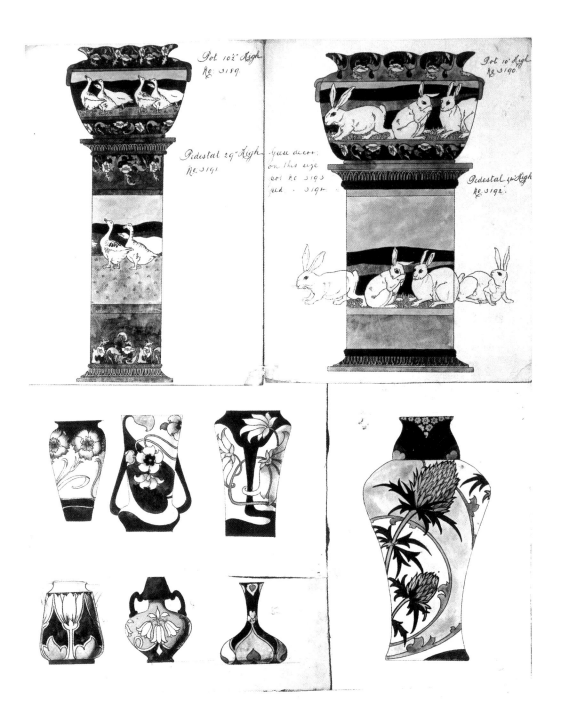

Intarsio designs from an original pattern book. The designs date from about 1900.

'Shelley's Fine China and Earthenware displayed in the new showrooms of Mr John Sayer . . .' Taken from the Pottery Gazette and Trade Record, March 1923.

designs of the earthenware ranges, Intarsio, Urbato, Pastello, etc, which made his reputation. What is perhaps less well known is the important contribution Frederick Rhead made to the surface design of the china wares, and to a whole range of utilitarian wares such as flowerpots, lamp bases, dessert and tea wares. Many shape designs were also added to the range during his period as Art Director.

All of Rhead's work, however, would not have even been given a chance to breathe had it not been for the direction and personal vision of Percy Shelley. Elevating the designer, at the expense of those responsible for their presence, is a seemingly subconscious failing of researchers, writers and collectors alike, a result of the effort to raise the status of the person behind the tangible objects that we love and desire to know more about. All too often, through repeated reporting in books, journals and articles dealing with the wares subsequent to their manufacture, the designer is placed on a pedestal, often rightly so, but often at the expense of those one stage removed from the ware. The owners, managing directors or works managers are the ones who orchestrate and hold together the whole scheme of things, making it possible to produce an end product at all. Percy Shelley, in this capacity, was determined that the only way forward for the pottery was through the production and promotion of good design and that by achieving these aims the pottery would lay down the foundation for a fruitful and successful commercial venture.

The first decade of the twentieth century saw two economic depressions in quick succession, the result of which was unemployment, reduced spending power and decreased output, largely as a result of short-time working. After the buoyancy, and consequent wealth, of the late nineteenth century which filtered unevenly through the classes, the rapid turn around in economic fortunes by 1902 was more than unexpected. As frequently and urgently reported in the ceramic and glass trade journals, the reason for this situation arose due to cheaper foreign goods flooding not only Britain but also those countries in which Britain had been trading successfully for many years.

The free rein given to Frederick Rhead had to be tightened considerably and what was needed was a return to safe and steady commercially acceptable wares. For this, Percy Shelley turned to Walter Slater, another man whose family was heavily involved in the Potteries as designers, artist and managers. Walter, following various members of the family, was trained at the Minton's pottery before going to work with his Uncle, John Slater, at the Nile Street Doulton works, where he remained for twenty years.

With little spare capital for experimentation Shelleys diversified into the making of china and earthenware of which Walter was put in charge. One of these diversifications was into the lucrative business of crested or heraldic china, a market explored by W. H. Goss, and taken up by Shelley in about 1903. In all there were in excess of four hundred shapes, applied with coloured transfer prints created by the in-house copper plate engravers. Nearly all of the models were numbered, which added to the appeal of trying to collect a complete set, numbers 1 to 120 used between 1903 to 1910. After the introduction of the new Shelley mark in 1910 the numbers started again at 130 and went up to 413 by about 1923. Between 1923 and sometime in 1924 production seems to have stopped as the lack of public interest, which had been waning for four or five years, led to the end of production, by which time Shelleys had got to number 511.

Walter Slater was also to supervise the design of patterns and shapes of various other wares including jelly moulds, advertising and commemorative wares. Only after 1910 did the economic circumstances of Britain and much of the rest of the world enable him to introduce more exotic wares. One of the ranges was in fact called 'Flamboyant ware' which involved the use of a flambé glaze. Walter also revived the previously popular Intarsio range, creating some very different designs with some reflecting the sinuous swirling lines of Art Nouveau, whilst others reflected more abstract classical motifs, more akin to the earlier work of the designer Dr Christopher Dresser. Numerous other styles, ranges and types of ware were developed during this period leading up to the first world war but perhaps some of the most significant were Walters designs for dinner and tea wares. The American market was very responsive to the new designs for the utilitarian chinawares, whether decorated with Japanese influenced patterns or Chinese inspired floral designs. This was the beginning of an important relationship between Shelley and the American market that was to sustain the pottery from the late 1930s through to the merger in 1966.

1910 was a significant year for the factory with the adoption of the Shelley China trademark that Percy Shelley initiated to distinguish Shelley wares from the other Foley potteries in Fenton and Longton (the pottery was actually within the boundry of Fenton although it used Longton as it's address). Of greater significance perhaps was that immediately after the war Percy was joined at the pottery by his three sons, two of whom, Percy Norman and Vincent Bob, returned from the war, whilst Kenneth Jack returned having completed his degree at Birmingham University. Each of the sons was given different tasks, most suited to their sensibilities, within the running of the factory, to which they all responded with enthusiasm.

The 1920s across the whole of British industry saw export markets being badly hit by abnormally high rates of exchange. Firms producing high priced luxury articles, as in much of the china industry, were heavily hit by much reduced orders due the high taxation being levied on those who would normally purchase such wares. In 1923 the trade press reported that with the exception of a "few factories in Longton which have been working five days

A collection of Mabel Lucie Attwell single figures with original boxes.

a week . . . the general average is three and a half to four days a week." Interestingly the tile industry was in an altogether far more cheerful mood, most firms having survived the complete stoppage of building during the war, being flooded with orders, some working overtime.

Towards the end of 1924 the trade press, (*The Pottery Gazette* and *Glass Trades Review*) whilst still relatively gloomy about the state of the pottery industry, with only moderate orders developing and a hand full of manufacturers even hinting at increased prospects. In September 1924, hope of some revival was found in the "craze for colour" which was very much in evidence in dress materials and millinery. "Pottery manufacturers have not been slow to realise the force of the new demand. Throughout the Potteries the showrooms are full of new designs in brilliantly contrasted colours – reds, yellows, greens – and very striking many of them are."

Two years later all hopes of any return to normal times were cast aside by the miners strike of 1926. In March there was still some hope of settling the dispute and unemployment in the Potteries was 6141, compared with 7524 for the same period in 1925. By the end of June, in the eighth week of the strike, unemployment had reached 27,331, with many factories closed and only a few making any sort of ware.

One of the many other things under discussion during this period was the new Merchandise Marks Bill. Percy Shelley was amongst those who thought that the bill did not go far enough, in terms of pottery, saying that he thought it ought to have a clause which stated that all pottery, whether manufactured in the British Isles or not, should all be indelibly marked. As the decade of the 1920s came to an end there was a final sting in the tail, as if the industry had not suffered enough, with the Wall Street crash of 1929, putting a final depressing touch to decade. As a consequence of events overseas there was a quite astounding proposal that 'all' the china manufacturers in Longton should 'combine' realising a capital of over £3,000,000. This plan was hatched by 'most members of the Longton Manufacturers who are members of the English China Manufacturers Association', which was basically all of those, who had already in principle agreed to the idea.

Exactly what factors were responsible for the most successful period of the Shelley Pottery, from the mid 1920s through to the second world war, would take some time to cover. As with any success story, a great deal depends on the foundations that had been laid before and Shelleys is no exception. The firm had been steadily growing and finding it's direction since the late nineteenth century, with significant contributions by the likes of Percy Shelley, Frederick Rhead, Walter Slater and more recently Jack Shelley. Jack Shelley was another in the mould of Percy Shelley, who worked enthusiastically and tirelessly behind the scenes promoting and advertising the name and wares of Shelley along every avenue he could possibly find. That the name and reputation of Shelley reached such heights during the inter-war years and even today is still very widely known and collected is in no small measure due to Jack Shelley's promotional schemes, as will be discussed in a later chapter.

What seems to set Shelley apart from those firms more used to the adulation and praise of being leaders in their field, for example Minton, Wedgwood, Doulton and Spode, is that their wares captured the spirit of the age. Diversity of design, which Shelleys had in abundance, and inventive new shapes, certainly immediately set the firm apart from many of their contemporaries. Another distinguishing feature of this pottery was that it had the foresight and business acumen, not to mention risk, of spending a considerable amount of its budget on advertising and promotion. Shelleys employed the best local firms to promote the pottery as well as cajoled retailers to go out of their way to sell the Shelley products, specifying numerous ways to achieve good sales and developing promotional material for the retailers. By "risk" think of the period under discussion here; the strike torn and depressed mid to late 1920s, followed by the Wall Street crash and all the subsequent faltering years. The *Shelley Standard* (as discussed in greater length elsewhere in this book) gives us a fascinating insight into some of the marketing and promotion methods used by the Shelley Pottery. It is for these reasons, amongst others, that the wares of the Shelley Pottery stand out from their contemporaries; years of toil, building and developing brought their just rewards.

That Shelleys was willing to be innovative and embrace new ideas and styles of design can be seen by the introduction of a new range of nursery wares, initially employing the services of Hilda Cowham in 1925, the success of whom brought the introduction of an even more well-known children's book illustrator, Mabel Lucie Attwell. As discussed in a later chapter, the success of the nursery ware ranges probably had as much to do with their appeal to the parents as well as a highly successful marketing campaign, than to any enthusiasm of those who were supposed to use the ware. Caution, however, is advised as the enthusiasm for these wares has not only brought high prices but also a few fakes, which are discussed in the 'Fakes' chapter.

1925 also saw the name of 'Shelleys' registered as the company trade name and by 1929 the pottery had become a limited company. As for the wares themselves, the next eight to ten years were to prove to be the making of the pottery, not solely for the innovative shapes and patterns, which provided the obvious, immediate visual appeal, but due also to the promotion, marketing and salesmanship that went on behind the scenes.

The first of the new shapes of the first of these innovative designs was the Queen Anne shape, introduced in August 1926 and in continual use until July 1933. This shape, together with the over 170 patterns used on it, put Shelley on the map, so to speak, the public quickly identifing the name of Shelley with this shape and vice versa. The shape was so highly regarded that in times of trouble, namely the 1950s, it was re-introduced with contemporary patterns being used until 1960 on Ideal china. In 1930 the boldest and most venturesome Eric Slater designs were launched by Shelley in the August, namely Vogue and Mode shapes.

At their initial showing critics in the trade press were sceptical, to say the least, about the impact and potential of such an obviously 'adventurous spirit'. The highly angular and geometric shapes of both these shapes, together with the specifically designed modern 'cubist' patterns, derives directly from the 1925 International exhibition held in Paris. The influence of this exhibition rapidly spread across to a wide variety of British firms. Unfortunately not all the firms showed much in the way of judgement or consideration when making use of the influence, most merely aping designs taken directly from carpets, textiles, furniture, etc, and repeating them on inappropriate wares. This severely devalued the meaning and impetus of the best of Art Deco (as it has become known), although one or two firms did manage to apply the principles and ideas of Art Deco to the medium with which they worked. Eric Slater's designs for Shelley show this balance and consideration in many, although not all, of the designs carried out for the Vogue and Mode shapes.

Although Vogue and Mode can be seen as successful statements of the era in which they were made, reflecting fashionable taste and ideals of the period, they were less successful as functional wares, receiving various criticisms about the width of the cups and the filling in of the triangular handles. Shelleys response was the introduction of the Eve shape in March 1932, with its bored-out triangular handles and slimmer shape. As a measure of the success of these wares one needs to look through the pages of the trade journals in the subsequent years to see numerous potteries producing extremely similar wares. Shelley themselves were not adverse to producing wares that owed much to another potter's wares, in one particular case those of the Moorcroft pottery. In this case however the Shelley wares were rather too similar. It was after William Moorcroft complained to Percy Shelley about the similarity of the Pomegranate decorated wares, designed by Eric, that they were withdrawn from production less than a month following their release in 1929. Enough pieces were made in that time to make them sufficiently rare to be quite highly sought after today.

A new decorative style was introduced in 1932. Called Harmony ware, this new style was to develop two distinctly different styles, the first being the use of overlapping bands of graduated shades of one colour or a combination of two shades of a colour. The other variation, known as dripware, involved the combination of two, three or four colours in a variety of band combinations and thickness, the essential ingredient being that one or two bands were applied with extra turpentine, to a precise consistency, in order to produce the important 'drip' effects. These effects were created, just as the bands were created, by turning the ware on a decorator's wheel at just the right speed and for the right length of time to allow both the drips to take effect and then the turpentine to evaporate, fixing the effect in place. At least this is something like the theory. The actual practitioners might have something different to say, this is however, how the Clarice Cliff 'bizarre' girls have recorded as the basics behind the effect. Clarice Cliff made use of the same idea on her Delecia ware as early as 1930, although without the spun effect. Eric Slater designed many shapes specifically to show-off the Harmony technique to its best advantage, the 'volcano' vase being a typical case. This range became so popular that there were at least twenty-five paintresses involved in the production.

The production and sales of Shelley were going exceedingly well, bolstered by the repeated advertising, promotion and marketing initiatives of all the Shelley family. As can be seen in a later chapter sales and orders were going rather too well if anything, with demand and orders exceeding production.

The mid 1930s, however, saw a change in fortunes, initially with the well-earned retirement of Percy Shelley in 1932, followed less than a year later by the sudden death of Jack Shelley whilst recovering from an operation in hospital. The effect on the family was naturally quite shocking, especially when Percy become ill shortly afterwards and died after a long illness in 1937. After these two great losses to the pottery Shelley china never really recovered. Loosing two pivotal figures, whose enthusiasm and awareness formed the focus of the pottery since the end of the First World War, combined with the dramatic alterations due to the second war proved too much.

Walter Slater, with the passing of his colleagues and most ardent supporters felt it was also time to leave the works having been art director there for thirty-two years. He had been grooming his son Eric to take over for sometime, in fact Eric Slater had, since the designs of the Queen Anne, and even more so, Vogue and Mode, been proving himself to be a more than adequate successor to his father. In 1933 Eric was elected onto the committee of the North Staffordshire branch of the Society of Industrial Artists, showing his maturity and enthusiasm for his position at Shelleys. A year after retiring and having seen his son fulfil his former role, Walter Slater died.

An Insight into the Successful Running of a Business

The history and name of Shelley is for most people synonymous with the wares produced in the 1930s. Shelley's managed to become a household name during this period, through the development and promotion of a seemingly endless choice of 'traditional' English patterns, in combination with contemporary highly-stylised abstract designs, but this was also the reason for their downfall. All too often a winning formula, in this case inexpensive bone china, which through the versatility and breadth of both shape and pattern which together with the use of the highly translucent fine bone china itself, all added up to something of seemingly greater importance, is adhered to for too long. The lack of any need for change was more often than not a consequence of customer demand, shapes such as Dainty White would only have been in production for so long due to continued demand, and much of that driven by overseas sales.

During the mid 1920s and 1930s much was being written and discussed about the virtues of good business sense, especially in the monthly ceramics and glass trade journals. Typically such topics advocated the encouragement of magazine advertising, potential of overseas markets and how to dress your windows to attract passing custom. Shelley were quick to respond with adverts appearing regularly in prominent positions in the ceramics and glass journals, all the more eye catching for having employed the services of W. H. Smedley, one of the most notable advertising agencies in Stoke-on-Trent.

Shelleys might have thought, as many businesses obviously did, that spending good money on advertising and promotion when there was have been little spare, was something of a luxury. It must be remembered that the 1920s was, and is still regarded as one of the worst economic decades of this century, with world political unrest and economic instability, especially in America, accompanied by massive unemployment. As far as the pottery industry was concerned things were bad enough for those firms with a heavy dependence on the export market, but even the manufacture of the ware itself became a problem due to the miners strikes, in particular the strike of 1926. Most potteries depended on coal to fire their kilns, therefore the lack of fuel supplies, which for some potteries dwindled to nothing for many months, meant the work force had to be laid off.

The vast majority of potteries, of a certain longevity, in Stoke-on-Trent, had had a relatively luxurious past, certainly until the early years of the twentieth century. Cheap foreign imports started to enter the country in vast numbers, seriously undercutting the prices of the British potteries, the resulting uproar being constantly reported in the trade press. If nothing else, what the dire situation provoked was a far healthier respect for the need to be beat the competition both in terms of price and quality, as well as in marketing and selling, making sure that any potential customers bought your wares and not your rivals.

Percy and Jack Shelley were particularly keen on developing new ways of marketing their wares, in fact as we have already seen from the 'Intarsio' wares produced at the turn of the century, promotion was something the Shelley pottery had always been keen on. One of the most immediately recognisable Shelley promotional schemes of the mid 1920s and 1930s was the 'Shelley Girl'. Developed by the Smedley advertising agency the 'Shelley Girl' was a 12 inch high model of an elegant young woman, seated, holding a cup and saucer in her left hand, wearing a white fox fur, red paisley style dress and black strap shoes. To top off the effect she wore a highly fashionable cloche hat under which tufts of her blonde hair protruded. In many respects this was a dream marketing image and was to prove so

Advert for Shelley's in the 1937 Pottery Gazette & Glass Trades Review, Directory and Diary.

for Shelley pottery.

The same 'Shelley Girl' appeared in various printed adverts during the late 1920s, her appearance often altering, until one of her last appearances, in 1930, when she was seen holding a Shelley cup and saucer, looking highly sensual and slightly dreamy, with the caption "Over the Hill" followed by "To the land of somewhere else, the kingdom of dream reverie . . . 'tis there that this Shelley pattern beckons us. On each dainty plate and cup, painted on the translucent white chinaware, is the Lovely road to bewitch the tea-time moment". If not pointing to the type of client that Shelleys were aiming to develop as customers, then certainly these adverts cultivated customers wishing to aspire to such a lifestyle. These figures would have been highly eye-catching either on the shop counter or as part of a window display, no doubt serving their purpose well. Recent research has indicated that the name of the woman who poised for the model of the 'Shelley Girl' was Elsie Harding.

An article by a West End display manager written for the *Shelley Standard*, "The Principles of Successful Window Display," even mentions the use of "special displays of the popular novelties of the moment . . . Pottery figures are another invaluable article for brightening the window display and imparting additional interest, and it is a sound policy to include in the windows some of the pottery modern opaque glass lamp standards. These may be so used as to assist the lighting."

Naturally these figures were made in very limited numbers, with only a certain number of retailers selling Shelley china, therefore to the collector they are rare and highly desirable. A word of caution, however, as rarity is often a bedfellow of restoration. In all the years that I have been looking at ceramics and of all the Shelley collectors I have spoken to, there are very few 'Shelley Girls' holding perfect cups, not to mention damage to the hats, skirts, etc.

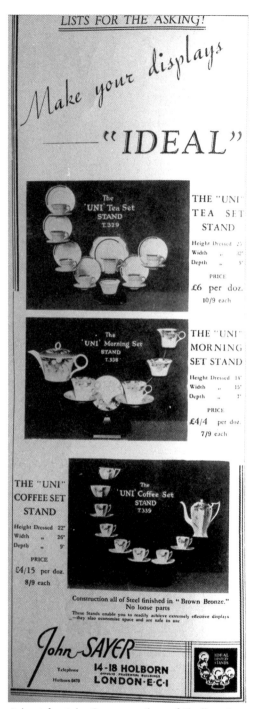

Advert for John Sayer, retailers of Shelley since 1923.

Remember these figures were used as daily display models and will inevitably have been picked up and put down many, many times.

Apart from the china figures there were also simple small name plaques, used to identify the manufacturer, with the name 'Shelley' in gilt. Other items that would expect to find on display on the counter, in the window and on the walls of a retailers were display boards and posters, each extolling the virtues of buying Shelley china. Some of the more interesting and innovative promotional wares, selling features and methods of advertising were promoted to shop keepers via an internal magazine called the *Shelley Standard*.

Whether this magazine was suggested by W. H. Smedley or an idea of Jack or Percy Shelley is not clear, but it has left us with is a wonderful insight into some of the promotional and advertising methods used by the Shelley factory to keep a cut above the competition. The *Shelley Standard* was produced bi-monthly between 1927 and 1931, and seemingly the only reason for the demise of the magazine was due to it's popularity and the wealth of orders that it generated, the warehouse being unable to cope with the demand. Shelley's were not the only pottery to start producing their own in-house magazine, but they were one of the first. What is noticeable, however, when the various company magazines, are compared, is the different slant that the *Shelley Standard* took when compared to the others.

To put things into perspective for a moment, the question could be asked, which other factories or makers were prominent during this period and how did they promote their wares? In terms of 'fashionable' tea, dinner and tableware there are of course Wedgwood, Doulton, Minton and such top-flight names. These firms, however, were largely content to rely on their name to sell their wares, the yearly round of trade fairs being the traditional time for displaying new lines and designs and the hard sales pitch. On a somewhat smaller but similar level of there are two individual names that immediately spring to mind, namely Susie Cooper and Clarice Cliff, the latter working for

A. J. Wilkinson Ltd. The former, being a relative newcomer to pottery ownership and with a limited budget for anything other than the tried and tested methods, was not heavily involved in the development of promotional side.

On the other hand the Wilkinson pottery under the guidance of Colley Shorter and head salesman, Ewart Oakes, had regular meetings, often weekly, to discuss advertising, promotion and sales. Clarice Cliff's designs were, of course, the main topic of conversation, although quite frankly her designs needed little additional promotion other than that frequently reported in the press, local and national, as well as various woman's magazines. In general, adverts placed in magazines, newspapers and trade journals lacked inspiration (excuse the pun for those Clarice Cliff readers) but then why spend lots of time and money on advertising when you could get press coverage for free. What Colley Shorter seemed to concentrate on was the secondary promotional effect, which came as a consequence of having some of the 'Bizarre Girls' sitting shop windows painting, banding and generally decorating for all the public to see. Displays in retailer's windows seemed to live up to the trade name of the ware itself, often quite bizarre and somewhat cluttered. Sophistication and delicacy were not something that was required to promote Clarice's wares as they were generally not aimed at that audience. The major difference concerning promotion and advertising at the Wilkinson works, and in this they were the pioneers, was that for first time in the pottery industry the name of the manufacturer was secondary to that of the designer, namely Clarice Cliff. This is something that was not contemplated at the Shelley pottery.

Returning to the *Shelley Standard*, this internal magazine in the early years was aimed at, for the most part, the employees. It covered internal developments within the pottery, as one would expect, reported on wakes weeks outings, the annual dinner dance, all with photographs, forthcoming marriages, births and deaths, clubs within the works, messages from the management and so forth. Later the editor(s), supposedly Jack and/or Percy Shelley, started to focus more attention on other readers of the magazine, namely their own retailers and stockists. One would have supposed that such stockists would automatically have been sent a copy of the magazine, thus developing that warm and friendly 'part of the family' good business approach. In any event new types of article started to appear, for example 'Building Business by Recommendation' by Thomas H Lewis, a member of the incorporated sales management association, with a section called "Word of Mouth Advertising". Mr Lewis was to be a frequent contributor to the *Standard* imparting useful advice to those who sold Shelley china.

Apart from the numerous articles concerning the running a business, management, sales, borrowing from the bank and related articles, all intended to help keep those selling Shelley wares in business, and most especially in the business of selling 'Shelley', some of the most frequent articles concerned window displays, promotions and advertising. For the most part the retailers had to do very little in terms of promotion and advertising, as the factory was more than willing to make-up displays, texts for advertising in local papers and, as we shall see, slides for the local cinema, figurines and retail books.

There were frequent illustrations of what a window should look like. "A cleverly designed window laid out in a dignified manner, well balanced, not only adds tone to your establishment, but is of the most forceful method of attraction available." Mr H R Jackson, of Bradford had "A special display of Shelley China . . . The stand was decorated in yellow and black, and the whole display was one of the most striking in the exhibition, and certainly one of the chief centres of interest. Two Shelley artists gave a display of painting." There were also ready-made displays "which can be obtained for use in your window. It is hand painted in full colours and measures three foot high by four foot wide when displayed. In addition to the screen illustrated here, which is 11618, we can supply screens with the following decorations – 11606. Chelsea – 11280. Iris – 115561. Crabtree – 11651. and Idaleum – 11652. If you would like the use of one of these screens, write to us saying decoration required and dates you wish to use it, as we have only a limited number to loan and early application is advisable."

The same idea with different adverts appears in July, September and November. By January 1931 a new scheme appears "if you wish to see new designs that are not stocked by the retailer ask to see designs in full colour in the beautiful Silver book or write for a copy of It, for your very own from Shelley . . ."

The new Silver book was first mentioned in the *Shelley Standard*, January 1931, the advert appearing at the back of the Standard. This Silver book was promoted as being full of all the varied Shelley china tea, coffee, morning and dinner sets that were to varied and numerous to be in stock at your local china merchants.

An interesting aside, in terms of advertising and promotion, was the typical attitude of the period towards women, as seen through the text and imagery of the adverts. Not only did the *Shelley Standard* have 'our woman representative' writing articles, but numerous illustrative articles with titles such as, 'Good China from a Woman's Point of View', 'Tea Table Harmony', 'We are Alive to the Fact' and 'Set out the Table', some of which are referred too later. Just a quick glance at where some, indeed most, of the advertising was placed also reveals much about the main target audience; *Good Housekeeping*, *Woman's Journal*, *Eve*, *Modern Home*, *My Home*, *Wife and Home*, *Woman and Home* (yes, there really were such titles), and *Britannia*.

Shelley's main line of wares were the very delicate, white, translucent bone china tea, coffee and dinner services, together with all the accompanying variations and sidelines that went with them. The person largely responsible for equipping the household during this period was the housewife, so whether it was her decision, a joint decision, or whether it was something that a couple was given as a wedding present, in matters of home furnishings it was the woman who held sway. Not unnaturally therefore, Shelley's advertising, through the professional agencies of Mr Smedley, was largely geared to developing new female customers and certainly those women who could afford to buy Shelley china. One way of achieving this aim was by keeping in touch with the latest fashionable society trends. "The vogue for the ensemble has spread from the toilet to the tea table, and the latest idea for the hostess who delights in dainty effect is china and linen, en suite for afternoon tea." (*Shelley Standard*, January 1930.)

The same article, which was stated as being 'Reproduced from a recent issue of the *Morning Post*,' continues. "The Iris forms the keynote for one fascinating scheme. On a background of creamy linen an Irish design is appliquéd which repeats the exact pattern and colouring on the china itself. The table napkins are en suite. The fairy lightness of the china, the delicacy of it's design and colouring, and it's thin, pearly translucent texture, are allied to the dainty, harmonising linen, achieved so novel and charming affect that the fashion bids fair to spread rapidly. If the Iris is not to ones taste, there are three other delightful Shelley harmony sets that may prove more to ones liking. The Daisy design is one of them. Delight to the eye. The corner of the old – world country garden, with clusters of gay flowers on a rustic arch, is reproduced on Shelley teasets that will delight the eye of the garden lover. It captures the spirit of the countryside, and though at present there is no matching table lay for this particular service, doubtless there soon will be." (*Shelley Standard*, January, 1930. "Tea Table Harmony by our woman representative." This was supposedly, if written by a woman at all, either Jack or Percy Shelley's wife, although this is merely an ideal thought.)

By September of the same year it was being reported that, "Owing to the great success of tablecloths to match Shelley teasets introduced last autumn, the manufacturers of the famous 'Buffalo' linen have now put five further patterns on the market. The patterns chosen include some of our most 'popular' stock patterns and all dealers stocking any of these lines should arrange with the local draper carrying 'Buffalo' branded linen to lend them the tablecloths so that they can be shown with the display of Shelley china. In case of any difficulty with the supplies of linen, the manufacturers, Messrs Robert McBride & Co. Ltd, 17 Cheapside, London. EC 2, will put china dealers in touch with drapers stocking these cloths, or if desired (and they have no customer in the neighbourhood,) sell the cloths and napkins to the pottery dealer. Of course the four patterns introduced last year to match Queen Anne, 11624, 11497, Vincent 11603 and Iris 11561 are still obtainable and are we are informed becoming as this new fashion is making rapid progress". Along with this there where four illustrations showing effect of the en suite linen.

This idea must have continued for several years with more patterns being added to the list, as the only such set I have personally seen, had the opportunity to buy and ever since very much regretted not buying (back in 1983), was a complete set of 'Polkadot' (sic) tea wares (introduced in July 1933) with six napkins and a table cloth. Shelley also turned their attention directly onto the customer in a variety of ways.

One of the 1930s adverts working on the principle of a 'free' give away for which the company got a useful 'free' list of potential clients, announced, "Beautiful china is acclaimed by famous hostess" which had picture of the Queen and some Shelley china. At the bottom it mentions "Free colour illustrations of Shelley tea, coffee, morning and dinner sets, nursery ware by Lucie Atwell. Dainty white china and jelly moulds stocked by leading china dealers, Shelley Potteries Ltd Dept, Longton, Staffs."

One of Shelley's most persuasive lines of promotion, in terms of encouraging Shelley stockists to place adverts in their own local press, was for Shelleys' themselves to place adverts in the national press, saying that in order to find out where your nearest stockist were, the local paper choeld be consulted. The stockists only had to write in to Shelleys for a free illustration to accompany an advert that had already been designed by Smedley to co-ordinate with the national press adverts, the stockists merely putting their own name and location on the advert.

In May 1930 another similar advert, with an illustration of tall trees, was discussed in the *Shelley Standard*. "Stocked by all the leading dealers. This message appears at the end of all Shelley advertisements and is address to readers of such papers as the *Daily Mail*, *Daily Express*, *Woman's Journal*, *Good Housekeeping*, *Britannia*, *Eve* and *Punch*, etc. The reader who is interested will ask his local china dealer for the goods advertised and is going to be disappointed if you cannot supply his needs. The enterprising dealer when buying new lines discriminates in favour of goods advertised, as he knows they will sell out faster and bring him greater profits. Send for illustrations of Shelley china to: Shelley Potteries Ltd, Longton, Stoke on Trent."

In the September 1930 issue, making sure to reach as many local people as possible, Shelley came up with the Shelley cinema advertising slide. "No matter what may be the opinion of the reader on the relative merits of silent and "talking" pictures the fact remains and it is plain to see that the cinema has taken a firm hold on the public imagination and nowadays one can hardly find a town without, the length and breadth of the isles, which does not possess its own picture palace." So stated the writer Thomas H. Lewis and he went on; "The cinema as a great educative force – That the cinema is a great educative force admits of no argument, it grips the attention, broadens the outlook and stirs the imagination as no other form of entertainment has ever done." . . . "The project of the picture or slide in the cinema theatre can have only one effect, to draw undivided attention; for the surrounding darkness is proof against the likelihood of eyes and interest being diverted from the screen. Assuming then – and we cannot fairly do otherwise – the spectator is in a receptive mood, the problem of the advertiser who desires to use cinema slides is so to use them that they do there work for him with the utmost efficiency. And so it is that, as in ever other form of advertising, screen publicity must observe the four basic steps of salesmanship: It must – 1 – attract the attention: – 2 – arose interest: – 3 – create desire: – 4 – move to action."

Just to ram the point home on the back of the same issue of the 'Standard', September 1930, was an advert showing the effect of the 'free' Shelley cinema slide. The advert reads – "Associate yourself with Shelley China national advertising. We shall be pleased to supply you with a special colour cinema slide incorporating your name and address free of charge. On condition that you undertake to exhibit it at your local cinema or theatre and by this you believe that from the many thousands of pounds spent by us to tell the public about Shelley China."

An important feature that seems to have been given a certain amount of attention in the pages of the *Shelley Standard* is "The Entrance of a Shop". In this interesting little article, Thomas H Lewis states that "the threshold being the final barrier between the customer and the shopper – will he cross that barrier? A sale depends upon his decision – perhaps his permanent custom may be the outcome. And so we come to understand why the shop door is a bigger consideration than a casual survey of the subject discloses."

In the same issue there is an illustration of a Shelley China door matt, with the text; "Have you a door matt? We are prepared to supply a limited number of solid rubber doormats; size 3' by 1'6" as illustrated above at a nominal price of 10 shillings each, these mats are normally worth 25 shillings. Why not order one at once, and thus link up your shop with the extensive advertising campaign now appearing for Shelley China? The white lettering is solid right through and the matt will wear for years." These mats were still being promoted in July 1931, when an order, related in the *Shelley Standard*, had been made on the strength of seeing the name on the doormat.

The Slow Decline

However successful Shelley's became as a consequence of the reputation and customer base they had developed in the 1930s it all came to an abrupt end with the outbreak of war. However not even a war could not stop the production of Shelley china. In the 1930s Shelleys developed a healthy export market so that by the time of the war, when the government was deciding which potteries to close, turn over to storage or production for the war effort, Shelley's, as with several other firms, was given special dispensation to complete foreign orders, thereby earning vital revenue. Production during the war was shared with their immediate neighbours, Jackson Gosling, trading under Grosvenor China, and production consisted mainly of Utility ware, as it became known.

In fact Shelley's had, unknowingly, pre-empted the need for plain inexpensive wares in May 1936 with the introduction of their 'Everybody Utility China'. For this new range they used a previously developed shape, Carlton, launched in 1925. On this occasion however, the wares were simply decorated with broad bands of green, blue, red and yellow on the exterior, with the same colours used on the handle and on a thin line inside the rim. These wares were promoted as being 'efficient, economical and practical', virtues which one of the great authorities of the period, Gordon M. Forsyth, had long been advocating, along with in his vilification of much commercial pottery production. For the war-time production of pottery, even the banded decoration had to go, the 'Utility' merely being left with the colour of the body, white, off-white and tones of ivory, or covered with a translucent or brown coloured glaze. The wares were marked with a rubber stamp using black ink, as were most of the 'Utility' wares, 'Shelley' over 'Grosvenor China' with 'and' in between.

During the war Shelley had continued to develop a healthy export market, especially in the USA, thanks to new designs such as 'Sheraton' which was specifically designed to satisfy the American desire for the 'antique-style' look that was their popular choice for U.S. interiors. In order to help the export drive, the government continued with the ban on home decorated pottery, established in 1942, until 1952. This inevitably caused a certain amount of stagnation in terms of new ideas and marketing impetus on the home front; and in some cases it led to unemployment and factory closures for those lacking export specialisation. There was also the problem of modernisation of equipment and development of materials, areas which languished on the back burner due to resources being taken up by more immediate concerns. Eventually, the sudden lifting of home market restrictions led to those manufacturers unprepared for the event having to solve innumerable problems of production, marketing and planning all at once. In the case of Shelley, concerns had largely been revolving around the continued production of export wares, which by the early 1950s accounted for something in the region of eighty per cent of their production.

In December 1945 the Shelley family as well as the firm suffered a great loss with the death of Vincent Bob Shelley. Vincent's role in family business had been mainly one behind the scenes but none the less important. A month later Eric Slater and the sales manager, Ralph Tatten, were elected to serve with Percy Norman Shelley, who became managing director, on the board of directors, to be joined by Alan Shelley, Vincent Bob's son, after he left the Navy in 1946. Two years later Alan's brother Donald joined the firm as technical director, having completed his degree in natural sciences at Cambridge University, at the same time becoming, with Alan the fourth generation to be involved in the business.

In the immediate post war period the British government were extremely keen to develop as much of an export market as possible, giving all kinds of financial as well as government support to achieve this. The simple reason was that Britain had a massive war debt owing to the United States, with still more America dollars needed to help rebuild British industry. As part of this incentive the Labour government set up 'development areas', usually where unemployment was highest, in which they would help finance and establish new developments, especially those projects set up by established firms.

At the same time the government wanted to promote good design both as an educational issue for the consumers as well as industry. In 1944 the Council of Industrial Design was formed, now the Design Council, with the aim of raising design standards in British industry and as a consequence improve British exports. One of its first initiatives was to pull together 5000 objects hastily gathered from industry up an down the country and mount the 'Britain Can Make It' exhibition in 1946, held at the then empty Victoria & Albert museum. Although promoted as displaying what would shortly be available in Britain following the lifting of manufacturing restrictions, in reality many of the objects were especially made for the exhibition or were prototypes for export or simply styles or shapes used before the war. The seven designs exhibited by Shelley fall into this sort of category, with six being designed by Eric Slater and one by an apprentice, Veronica Ball, the stylised leaf and foliate motifs of these designs being more akin to something Susie Cooper might have done ten years earlier.

Further high profile educational events were planned, the biggest being the 'Festival of Britain' in 1951. Much has been written in subsequent years mostly in praise of this event, its significance, influence and the regenerative powers that grow as consequence of the nationwide showing and exhibitions that were part of the Festival. Unfortunately, such claims have recently been tempered following the realisation that much of the post-festival congratulatory and back slapping press was written by many of those involved in the setting up and running of the festival. Subsequent writings in more recent years seem to have fallen on this literature and perpetuated the same sentiments. In retrospect, some products and consumer goods, wallpapers, textiles, some furniture and some ceramic wares, were repeatedly picked on by the press, during the 1950s, as extolling the virtues of the 'contemporary' and 'new' life style of the young. Unfortunately these wares tended to be the products of small firms with low-volume turnover that sought the high-profile fashionable image and therefore had little serious impact on the mass consumer.

Eric Slater, who was 50 in 1951, had long been an advocate and supporter of the renewed interest and debates promoting the virtues of good design, aimed at both the consumer and industry. In 1951 Eric appeared amongst a distinguished panel of 'experts', at the request of the ceramic industries main trade journal and voice, the *Pottery Gazette and Glass Trade Review*, to participate in a 'Design Quiz' which was to answer over a number of weeks twelve frequently asked questions on design. Some of the questions put regarded the training of designers, 'good' design and 'bad' design, 'specialisation leads to better designers', and question four, have the Council of Industrial Design (COID) made their objectives clear to the pottery industry?

Unfortunately, whilst Eric was involved in such debates, there seemed to be little movement back at the Shelley pottery in answer to many of the questions being posed. When Eric Slater designs for Shelley are compared with the designs of Colin Melbourne at Wade and Beswick, Jessie Tait for Midwinter and other designers working at Hornsea, Poole pottery, Ridgway, Spode and even the nearby Foley Bone China works of E. Brain & Co., between 1950 and 1955, the different approaches are very apparent. In the trade journals for 1951 Shelley were still advertising the 'Sheraton' design from the early 1940s, not to mention Dainty White rather traditionally decorated with scattered flowers. 'Hedgerow' was another

Part of the decorating shops at the Shelley works. A copy of this photograph was used in the trade jounral Pottery & Glass in March 1959.

of the designs being alternately advertised with 'Sheraton'. During 1953 Shelley advertising all but dried up in the face of heavy competition from the new 'contemporary-styles' being promoted by the new fashionable potteries.

At this crucial period in the history of the Shelley pottery there was a cultural shift towards a younger generation with a far larger disposable income than they had had before the war. Shelley's, in hindsight, would have done well to employ today's equivalent of an outside consultancy to revamp their image and house style, which is exactly what companies like Midwinter did. The new young consumers had a high level of disposable income, as well as a very different set of expectations and desires in terms of home furnishings, life style and eating habits. To a large extent this was brought about by glimpses of what was available in America, albeit glorified, and staged through magazines, radio and the beginnings of television. The young desired to get away from the past and the expectations of previous generations. This was reminiscent of the years following the First World War and the lively jazz age that followed.

Bone china as a material was generally accepted as being symbolic of good taste, refinement, lavishness and delicacy, not to mention having its associated behavioral patterns of calmness, elegance and sedentary characteristics. These were not attributes with which the numerous 'twenty-somethings', setting up home in the 1950s wanted to be associated. Bone china in the post-war period was, seen by the young as something, that the previous generations would have had either in a display cabinet and used on special occasions, or brought out only for afternoon tea. The very nature of the material, bone china, further implies certain longevity of use and refinement. Shelleys were aware of this, their best selling patterns being 'classic' timeless designs that would be used for many years.

One could, looking back through the history of the Shelley pottery, point to the 'Queen Anne', 'Vogue', 'Mode', 'Regent' and 'Eve' shapes and some of their more abstract 'Art Deco' patterns as being examples that seemingly contradict the accepted values associated with bone china as a material as mentioned above. These shapes and patterns, however, as stated previously, were aimed at and largely bought as fashion statements and wedding presents in the 1920s and 1930s, by well to do or young twenty-something's setting up house for the first time. Newly weds and the young single, again desiring something completely different from previous generations and something that reflected the bright and bold primary colours and abstract patterns typical of continental styles of the period, found in the Shelley patterns and shapes what they wanted. Something reflecting their social standing, and at the same time reflecting their fashion awareness and sensibilities, was what mattered.

The reaction of other potteries to the demands of the new consumer, namely the young, was to employ the best new young graduates; many from the Royal Collage of Art, and from 1950 onwards there seemed to be a steady stream. These designers were to find a new and unrivalled freedom in the design studio of a very limited number of potteries such as, Midwinter, Poole, Spode, Wade, Hornsea, Denby and Foley China amongst others.

Great developments were being made at Shelley but these were of a highly technical nature under the guidance of Donald Shelley. Indeed it seems quite likely that an increasing proportion of the firm's resources were being taken up by the introduction of new machinery as well as actually developing new machinery themselves. The great challenges of the period came about through the government's desire to see vastly improved working conditions. One of the main causes of concern was the hundreds of bottle kilns, often a handful or more at each pot bank, belching out clouds of black smoke from the coal fired kilns. Various technical developments and inventions had been made during the twentieth century to improve on the ancient bottle kilns, one of the earliest being the Dressler continuous firing

Tunnel Oven, developed in 1905 with the first working kiln installed in 1910. Not every pot bank, however, had the space for a one hundred and twenty-foot long kiln, let alone the resources to finance it. In 1950 at Shelleys a new glost kiln was installed which resulted in far fewer losses during the firing and an improvement in the quality of the ware. Two years later Donald Shelley had developed and patented an 'ingenious cup-casting machine which produces one cup every ten seconds' as reported in a special article, 'The Shelley Story', in the 1959 *Pottery and Glass Record*. One of the main assets of this machine, developed in conjunction with Mr Scholefield of the Midlands Electricity Board and operation until 1967, was that cups were produced with an overall consistent thickness, not readily achievable through hand turning. Donald Shelley's main technical achievement, the prototype in operation in 1955, was to have a significant effect on the production of the ceramics industry, at least for those that invested in it. This was the top hat kiln.

Just as the Conrad Dressler continuous firing tunnel oven and its subsequent related developments began the demise of the bottle kiln, so the top hat kiln can be seen as the culmination in terms of space saving, fuel economy and efficiency, as well as quality, that finally saw the end of the bottle kiln. If it failed in any respect it was in lack of volume. The solution to this was merely to have enough kilns, each with two bases, to keep in-line with capacity requirements. By the end of 1956 eight top hat kilns with sixteen bases were in constant use at Shelley. The Shelley family, realising the importance of this kiln established the Shelley Furnaces Ltd company in May 1956 so that, once they had built enough kilns for their own use, they could start selling them to other manufacturers. More than anything else it was the government's forced introduction of the clean air act, along with many other health and safety policies, that made manufacturers introduce new machinery and equipment, as well as altering some working practices.

Developments were also being made in other fields, mostly in an effort to increase production rates with either the same or a reduced work force. Lithographic transfers were used significantly during this post-war period, technical developments having brought about brighter and bolder colour palettes as well as far better quality through the refined use of silk-screen printing linked with photography. The use of transfers reflected an economic necessity for volume production but at the expense of quality, indicative perhaps of a change in the customer base, as has been mentioned before. The costs involved in hand-painting were by the late 1950s very high, taking any such decorated wares almost invariably into the luxury market. Why exactly Shelleys should decide to revive the labour intensive nineteenth century sgraffito lustre wares, in the 1950's, is something of a mystery, especially in light of the direction of fellow manufacturers. This revival was short lived and appears to have been linked more to some experimentation work Eric Slater was associated with at the Burslem School of Art.

The only significant research and development in the design department during the last years of the Shelley pottery was, in hindsight, far too late and lacked confidence. The introduction of the new and innovative Sterling shape in July 1956 has to be seen in context as Shelleys were still making and selling the Regent, Gainsborough and, of course, Dainty shapes. Any visitor to the factory must have been highly confused at the incongruous mixture of ancient and modern. The Sterling shape evolved out of a direct influence of the importance of the American market. It is perhaps interesting to note that Michael Farr, author of the exhaustive book *Design in British Industry*, published in 1955, noted that during a visit to nineteen potteries in 1952, fourteen of them had started to manufacture shapes influenced by the 'coupe' form, a shape then in production in America although originally from Scandinavia.

Having looked at the pattern books for the last few years of production under the Shelley title, it is not surprising to feel a sadness tinged with frustration and not a little disbelief, as the pages are turned. What will be found, if you leaf through the 1960s pattern books, is a slightly confused company, steeped in the past, or rather perhaps capitulating to the demands of the consumer, both in the UK and abroad, yet making some effort, though not enough, to move with the times. Inevitably it was relying on the safety of what they knew best that was to spell their own downfall. With all due respect to the then loyal company team in a highly competitive business and, of course, with the benefit of hindsight, one thing that Shelley seemed to be crying out for in the 1950s and 1960s was new energy and ideas.

At a time when other companies were producing between five and ten new pattern designs as well as new ranges every year, all reflecting the highly fashionable contemporary tastes of the period, Shelley following the war produced only a few new shapes, 'Sterling' and 'Avon'. This is not including a one-off special order of a very large cup and saucer, 'Ovide', for the overseas market. There was, of course, strong competition from potteries in Japan, Germany and other European countries many of whom benefited from significantly reduced labour wages and more modern equipment, all of which hit export sales of British companies. Shelley's export sales during the 1950s, while still accounting for seventy to eighty percent of overall production, fell until the early 1960s. Looking through the trade journals from for the whole period between 1950 to the take-over in 1966, Shelley's seemed to show less and less interest or commitment as the 1950s era progressed. Advertising all but ceased, 'Wild Flowers' being advertised in the *Pottery Gazette and Glass Trades Review* of February 1957, the next extremely sparse and thin advert, 'Anemone', appearing in February 1960. In the sister trade journal the *Pottery and Glass Record* there are literally no advertisements during the late 1950s and the only time Shelley merits a mention is either because of the top hat kiln or in a special article on the pottery, as if by way of a testimonial before the inevitable end.

The importance of the American and dollar

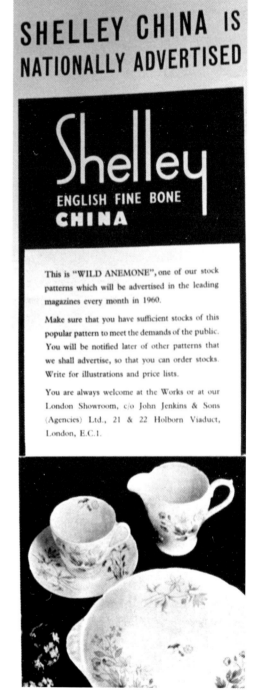

A Shelley Potteries Ltd advertisement in 1960 for Wild Anemone.

markets to the firm cannot be underestimated. In a specific article about Shelley, entitled 'The Shelley Story' (*Pottery and Glass*, March 1959.), written in the wake if the Blackpool Trade fair, the whole theme is one of dependence on the dollar markets. When talking about the immediate post war period the author of the article explains that "the making of bone china dinnerware for the dollar countries was given first priority, and this became the firm's most important asset". Later on in the article it caries on, "Over one-third of the firm's ware is destined for the United States, 80 per cent of their total production being exported". A little later we are given the popular patterns with 'Golden Harvest' and 'Bridal Wreath' being particularly popular in the United States, as well as 'Trousseau' in rose. The latter pattern in celeste or sylvan green was popular in Canada. Another new design of the period (1959) was 'Columbine' on the Sterling shape that sold very well in Bermuda to the visiting Americans, along with the souvenir giftwares. Not to be forgotten, in terms of the American market, was the highly popular 'Dainty White' shape which was selling 'extremely well' with the 'Bridal Rose' design described as "a truly feminine pattern."

On the home front we find that, not surprisingly, floral patterns are the most popular, namely 'Wild Flowers' and 'Charm', with 'Field Flowers' and 'Syringa' being two new designs introduced at the Blackpool fair.

When examining at the various firms that were advertising heavily during this period and what they were producing, it is clear to see not only the dependence Shelleys had on their export market but also how out of fashion they had become. By this time Poole pottery, Midwinter, Denby, Ridgway and Spode were making high fashion ranges, Midwinter's being the leaders in this field employing several young contemporary designers.

Late in 1964 within the last eighteen months of the production of Shelley the last cup shape, Avon, was introduced. Having seemingly missed out of making a new 'contemporary' shape in the 1950s, Shelley produced a typically stylish and up to the minute contemporary shape of the 1960s. It was however too little too late, symptomatic of post-war Shelley. Several designs were registered for this shape, the most stylistic and compatible being 'Blue' and 'Pink Harlequin' in October 1963, 'Naples', 'Apollo' (illustrated on page 96) and 'Aegean' (illustrated on page 96) in 1964 and 'Mosaic' in 1965. Although heavily based on the award winning Spode manufactured and Royal College of Art designed shape, initially named 'Royal College' and later changed to 'Apollo', which in turn shows the influence Eva Zeisel works, the Shelley 'Avon' looked set to launch Shelley back into prominence. Unfortunately it was never given the chance, in the first instance due to a lack of concentrated publicity but mainly because of the take over of the Shelley pottery in mid 1966. That Shelley's were, even at the closure, still highly dependent on the American market and led by the tastes of the consumer can be seen by glancing at the last twenty or thirty pages of the pattern books. The pages are filled with numerous Chintz patterns – Green Chintz, Daisy Chintz, Blue Chintz, etc as well as numerous other retrospective patterns one would more normally associate with the 1920s and 1930s.

Only a year previously Shelley Potteries Limited changed their name to Shelley China Ltd, perhaps in an effort to inject some impetus into the products or perhaps merely to galvanise themselves into greater efforts. The reality was that the business environment was changing, it was becoming harder for family run firms to keep pace with new marketing strategies, projected growth figures, market research and the new approaches the younger generation of business management professionals were developing. Shelley's had to watch as numerous companies around them were taken over in the post war period, with more marked aggression in the mid-1960s. The aggressor being the financial holdings company, S. Pearson & Sons Ltd and Shelley, after the likes of Colclough's, Lawley's, T.C. Wild and Royal Crown Derby, become another of the take-overs in mid 1966.

Norman Shelley never quite saw the final blow to the pottery as he died in May 1966 at the age of seventy-two. In 1964 the group of potteries under the wing of Pearson's become known as Allied English Potteries and following the take-over of Shelley's the works was set up to make Royal Albert wares, the name of the works changing to Montrose. As a consequence you can find Royal Albert shapes with Shelley backstamps and patterns, but after a short while these were used up along with the mark of Shelley.

Shortly after the disappearance of Shelley wares from the market it become clear that the market for china export ware had a huge gap that proved impossible to fill for many years. Such was the impact of taking out of the export figures the unique position Shelley's had developed since the 1920s. It has been pointed out although Shelley as a pottery is no longer in existence the name of Shelley lives on. The Royal Doulton pottery was making nil returns filed at Companies house, thereby keeping the name alive.

In many ways during the post-war years Shelleys, as a company, did not help their own situation by concentrating on the export market only and diversifying into technological areas that were not their true specialisation. The situation in the potteries during this period was not helped by cheaper foreign competition, many newly established firms having the latest technological equipment, rising costs of materials and labour costs, and radical changes in working conditions. The government brought in numerous health and safety measures, the most radical being the introduction of the clean air act, forcing manufacturers to cease coal firings, leading to the expense of alternative methods. Shelleys were, more than anything else, a victim of changing market and social expectations during the post war period, with a move away from the traditional materials to those more in keeping with changing life-styles. Even with all the market research, new managerial skills and key economic rationales seemingly required to make a business work and develop in the 1960s, it would have been difficult for Shelleys to re-equip for production in another material, which might have rekindled the fortunes of the firm.

An original design for an umbrella stand, no: 3223, with panels of large flowers and elongated foliage on an olive green ground.

A large Urbato clock case, decorated with the 'Hickory Dickery Dock' nursery rhyme. Tube-lined lettering and outlining, with a sgraffito colouring effect. £800-£1200/$1560-$2460.

An Intarsio ware vase, decorated with a broad panel of an Egyptian woman wearing an elaborate headdress, amongst tall flowers and foliage, £600-£800/$1170-$1640.

A two-handled Intarsio ware vase, decorated with an Egyptian figure kneeling with outstretched winged arms, £400-£600/$780-$1230.

A large Intarsio ware triple plant holder, the wavy rimmed neck decorated with a band of fish swimming amongst the waves, £800-£1200/$1560-$2460 (£300/$575 for a restored one in 1996).

A tall Intarsio ware double-handled vase, decorated with a panel of St Cecilia standing in long flowing robes, a triple lappet band below, repeated above, £500-£700/$975-$1435.

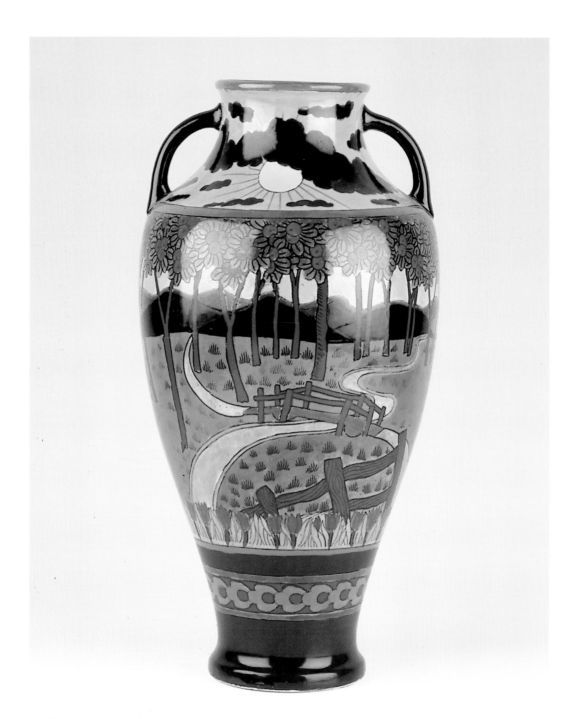

A tall two-handled Intarsio ware vase, decorated with a landscape panel of a meandering stream and wooden fence in the foreground, tall thin trees in front of mountains in the distance, £800-£1200/$1560-$2460.

Left: An Intarsio ware vase, decorated with a continuous band of witches on broomsticks, £400-£600/ $780-$1230. Right: A tall vase with a continuous band of green pixies, below a band of owls. £600-£800/$780-$1640.

Top: An Intarsio ware vase, with a Shakespearean scene of Ariel riding on the back of a bat, a moon behind and Puck sitting on a toadstool on the reverse, £300-£500/$585-$1025. Bottom: An Intarsio ware flask decorated with a Shakespearean scene of a turreted castle on one side and Macbeth holding a sword on the reverse, £300-£500/$585-$1025.

An Intarsio ware vase decorated with a Shakespearean scene, £500-£700/$975-$1435.

An Intarsio ware vase decorated with a continuous band of elderly gentleman's heads sucking on pipes enveloped by clouds of smoke, £500-£700/$975-$1435.

A Middle Eastern influenced Intarsio ware teapot, decorated with bands of stylized flowers on the compressed double gourd body, a repeated floral band on the high domed lid. £500-£700/$975-$1435.

A large Intarsio ware clock case, the central panel decorated with sail boats on a river with tall stylized lily flowers in the foreground, flanked by two panels, one with a female figure holding a lily, the other holding a lamp, a crescent moon behind her head, £1200-£1500/$2340-$3075.

An Intarsio ware mantel clock case, in the form of a grandfather clock, decorated with quartered open flower-heads around the clock face above a panel of a female figure blowing on a dandelion, with an inscription 'Prithee What O'Clock', £800-£1200/$1560-$2460 (£450/$875 in 1993-94).

An elaborate middle Eastern influenced Intarsio ware jug, (left) the disc body decorated with the head
of a woman wearing a helmet, with bands of stylized flowers and snowdrops, £500-£700/$975-$1435.
An Intarsio ware two-handled vase, (right) decorated with a broad band of repeated mermaids. £400-
£600/$780-$1230.

The reverse of illustration from previous page.

An Intarsio ware vase, decorated with a band of ladies in medieval dress walking on a bridge with irises below, £600-£900/$1170-$1845.

An Intarsio ware two-handled vase, decorated with angels behind an open panelled wall, tiled roof, tulips in the foreground, £600-£900/$1170-$1845.

A large Intarsio ware wall plaque, depicting in the centre, two women wearing classical dresses, one playing the lyre the other sewing, within a broad band of Art Nouveau style flowers and foliage, £800-£1200/$1560-$2460

An Intarsio ware wall plaque, the centre depicting an angel holding lilies, the sun behind her, within a broad band of compartmentalised renaissance-style foliage alternating with a trellis band, £600-£900/$1170-$1845.

A tall Intarsio ware vase, (left) decorated with a castle in the distance, tall black tress in the foreground, with a bird in flight above on a band around the neck, £700-£900/$1365-$1845. On the right a tall two-handled vase, decorated with a continuous band of geese between stylised foliate bands, £700-£900/$1365-$1845.

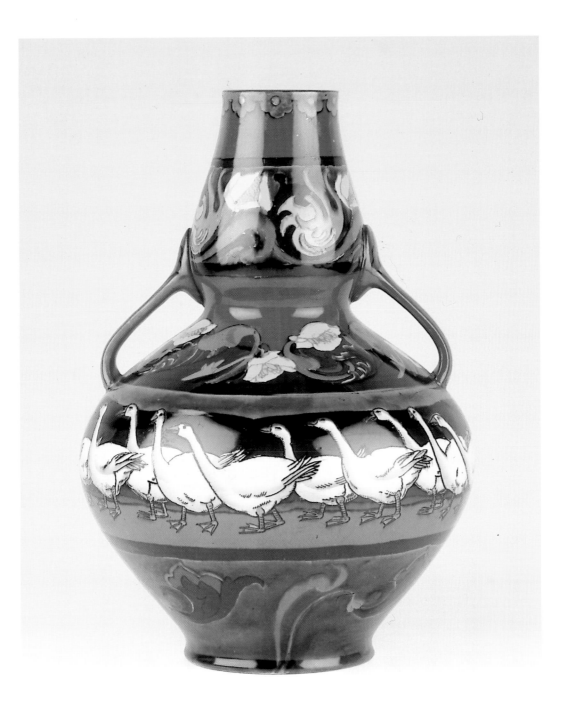

A tall Intarsio ware two-handled vase, the bulbous body decorated in a similar fashion to the previous vase, £700-£900/$1365-$1845.

An Intarsio ware Middle Eastern-style teapot, decorated with a band of swans around the bulbous body with bull rushes on the narrow neck, £700-£900/$1365-$1845.

A bulbous four-handled Intarsio ware vase, decorated with a continuous band of chickens and chicks, between entrelac bands, a band of buttercups around the neck, £700-£900/$1365-$1845 (£400/$750 in 1993).

A Harmony ware vase, circa. 1937. The body showing deliberate imitation of hand-thrown ribbing although these pieces were made in moulds. In fact, you could choose to have ribbed or flat sided wares. £70-£100/$135-$200.

An Intarsio ware vase, the compressed ovoid body decorated with swans, their necks extending to the narrow neck, £200-£400/$390-$820.

Top left: an Intarsio ware vase with a wide flared mouth, decorated with a continuous band of penguins, a lappet band on the rim, and top right: showing the base, £400-£600/$780-$1230. Bottom: A long Intarsio ware rectangular plant holder, decorated with a continuous band of rooster, hens and chicks, £400-£600/$780-$1230.

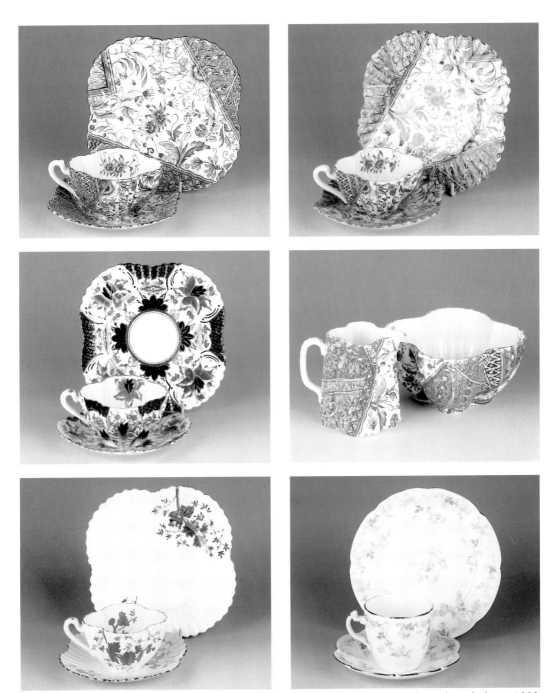

All Alexandra shape, except bottom right, registered November 1886 and used until about 1902, £40-£90/$80-$185. The right bottom design Lily, introduced in 1888 and still in the pattern books in 1918, £30-£60/$60-$125.

Top left is another Lily shape, £30-£60/$55-$125. Top and middle right is the Daisy shape, registered in the same year lily was introduced, 1888 and was last recorded in 1913, £30-£60/$55-$125. Bottom left and right, is the Fairy shape, which was in use for five years, from 1890 to 1895, £30-£60/$55-$125. The remaining illustration on this page, middle left, looks very like Daisy next to it but has a twist in the lobed body and does not seem to be identifiable, £30-£60/$55-$125.

Daisy continues from the previous page, top left, this time returning to the completely covered Japanese influenced designs we saw on the Alexandra, £30-£60/$55-$125. The remaining illustrations of this page, with the exception of the bottom left, are all in the Empire shape, introduced in 1893 and still in the pattern books in 1910. Bottom left is the exotic Shell shape, used between 1891 and 1894, £30-£60/$55-$125.

Top two and middle left shapes are again in the Empire design. The middle left design shows a heavy use of the 'Imari' palette, £40-£80/$75-$165. Another new shape is Century, right middle and bottom left, which was in use between 1895 and about 1902, £30-£60/$55-$125. On the bottom right is Dainty, perhaps the most famous shape Shelley produced and without a doubt the longest in production, £40-£80/$75-$165.

Registered in 1896 the Dainty shape, designed by Rowland Morris, was still in production some seventy years later in 1966. £30-£150/$55-$310. At the bottom right is the highly stylized Snowdrop shape. £30-£60/$55-$125.

The Snowdrop shape, used between 1896 and 1914, highlights the sweeping curves of the Art Nouveau style of the period in the top two illustrations as well as the middle left, £60-£120/$115-$245. The middle right and bottom left, displaying the Japanese influence, £40-£80/$75-$165. In 1899 Violet was introduced, bottom right, £30-£60/$55-$125. Violet was introducèd as an alternative to the Fairy shape seen on page 60.

Top left is another Violet shaped trio, £30-£60/$55-$125. This is followed, top right and middle left, by two transfer printed patterns, this time of overlapping floral swags, in two colour-ways on the Court shape, used between 1906 and 1913. Six years after the pottery began trading under the name 'Shelley China' (1910), the Vincent shape was introduced, middle right and bottom left, and was to be home for over 200 patterns until 1933, £30-£60/$55-$125. Bottom right is the shape that made Shelley a household word, Queen Anne, here seen with the 'My Garden' design introduced in 1928, £40-£90/$75-$185.

The next two pages are devoted to the Queen Anne shape, with more illustrations on other pages. If nothing else this indicates how prolific and popular this shape was, selling to many countries around the world. Introduced in August 1926, it held over 170 patterns until 1933, its official withdrawal. The shape was re-introduced in the 1950s and was certainly being used on Ideal china until 1960. The 'Blue Iris' design, bottom left, is the most sought after, £100-£150/$195-$310.

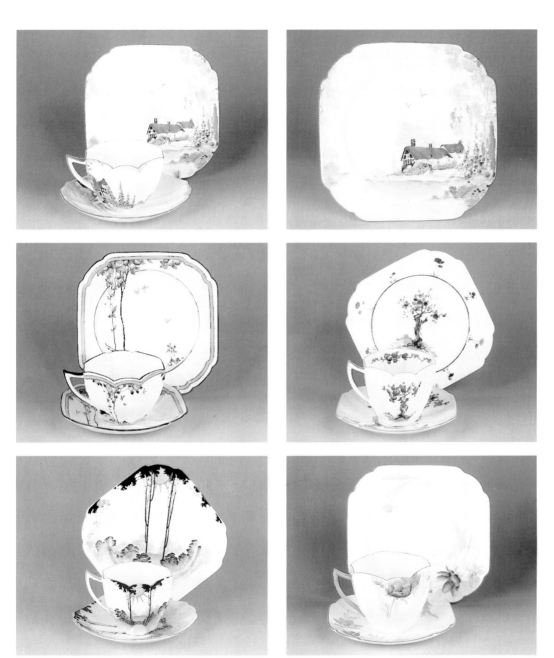

More of the Queen Anne shape, the top two illustrations, 'Cottage – 2', introduced in September 1928, reflect the tastes of the buying public, even if the design is somewhat unhappy on the shape, £50-£80/$95-$165 (for the trio). Middle left is 'Balloon Trees' £70-£100/$135-$200 and next to that on the right is 'Crabtree', £70-£100/$135-$200. One of the most successful and sought after designs is 'Sunset and Tall Trees' £100-£150/$195-$310 which seemed to outlast most of its contemporary designs.

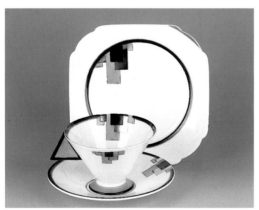
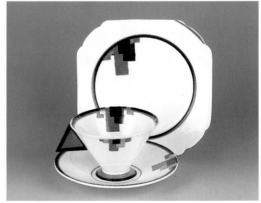

Here on the top left is a rather difficult one to spot, having a 'Cloisonné' style pattern, seemingly dating from 1916-17 on a Queen Anne shape, £30-£60/$60-$125. Similarly with the Blue Bird design, £20-£40/$40-$80. Here we have the height of fashion with Vogue, £100-£150/$195-$310, middle left, and Mode, £100-£150/$195-$310 middle right, both introduced in 1930. The designs here influenced by continental art, namely Cubism and Art Deco.

Top left: Vogue with the 'Butterfly Wing' £120-£180/$235-$370; Top right: Mode decorated with the 'J' design £100-£150/$195-$310; Middle left: Eve was a new shape launched in March 1932, because of comments about the above two designs, £80-£120/$155-$245; Middle Right: a typical simplistic Art Deco pattern on the Vogue shape £60-£90/$115-$185; Bottom left: we can see a change of direction with the introduction of the Regent shape in September 1932, £80-£120/$155-$245; Bottom right: the Oxford shape, introduced in 1934 running concurrently with Regent, lasting until 1939, being specifically developed to be used for coffee, £60-£90/$115-$185.

The top four designs here are in the Henley shape a new design in August 1938, disappearing by 1940. The top two illustrate a move to lithographic decoration, £40-£60/$80-$125. The middle left is a timeless classic based on the light scattering of the 'Elizabethan Rose' style design popular since the late nineteenth century, £40-£60/$80-$125 The complete opposite of this is the middle right design which smoothers the whole surface, £40-£60/$80-$125. The final trio Perth, was introduced either to replace Regent, or to harmonise with Henley, £40-£60/$80-$125.

A Mode shaped Coffee set, circa 1931-32, decorated with a large red block overlapped by a smaller black block, £400-£700/$780-$1435.

Part Sunray tea set on the Vogue shape, 1930-33, £500-£700/$975-$1435 for pieces illustrated. (Same number of pieces with teapot made £1100/$2145 in 1996).

A collection of mainly Queen Anne cream and milk jugs, with a dainty cream jug at the top and an Violet jug at the bottom right. Prices range between £40-£90/$80-$185.

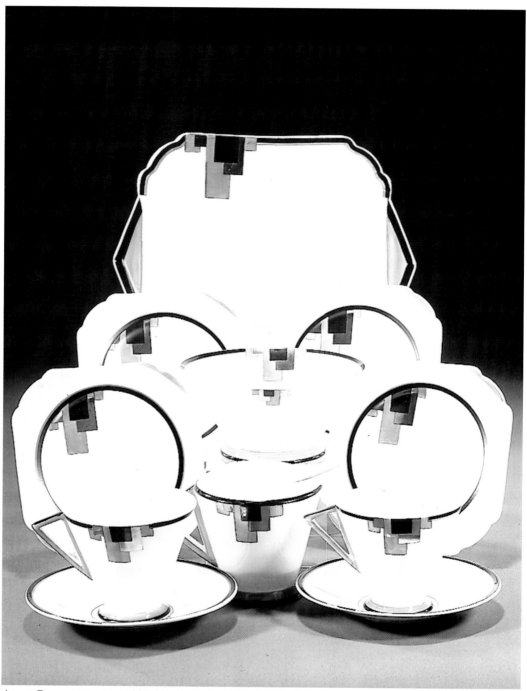

A part Eve tea set, circa 1932-33, decorated with the Blocks pattern originally designed for the Vogue shape in 1930, £350-£550/$685-$1130.

A part 'Anemone' tea set (top), introduced in 1932, on the Queen Anne shape. One of at least seven colour variations, £250-£350/$490-$715. Bottom is 'Blue Iris' pattern on the same shape, £300-£500/$585-$1025 (£400/$750 in 1994 coffee set, six cups and saucers).

Top: a part Regent coffee set, with the Oxford shaped cups, therefore dates between 1934 and 1939, £250-£350/$490-$715. Below is a very unusual lemonade set, seemingly based on the Vogue shape. This is one of four designs that appear in the 'Specials' pattern book, all dated 1931, £250-£350/$490-$715.

A group of Queen Anne teapots, £250-£350/ $490-$715 and one Vogue teapot £300-£400/$585-$820. Worth noting are the two splendid tea pot stands, top and bottom, as well as the variations in size.

Part Butterfly Wing tea set on the Mode shape, 1930-31. £400-£600/ $780-$1230 (for pieces illustrated).

Top left is a 'Crabtree' pattern Queen Anne coffee pot, £200-£300/$390-$615 with a matching comport below (bottom left). £30-£50/$60-$105. Top right is a 'Balloon Tree' Queen Anne cake plate and matching hot water jug, with a hinged metal cover that swings open as you pour, hopefully, £100-£150/$195-$310. Bottom right is a cased abstract patterned part coffee set on the Eve shape, with bean-end spoons. This should in fact have another cup, center back, with three saucers in a row. £400-£600/$780-$1230 (as a complete set).

This lady curtseying dates from the 1930s and is very rare as very few were made, £300-£500/$585-$1025.

A colourway of the previous lady curtseying, again dating from the 1930s, £300-£500/$585-$1025.

Again this figure of a Lady in a crinoline dress was made during the 1930s and was not produced in any great number, £300-£500/$585-$1025.

The Moorcroft-style vase is just that, an imitation of the Moorcroft Pomegranate pattern, £300-£500/$585-$1025.

A selection of Mabel Lucie Attwell Nursery ware designs – A hot baby plate £80-£120/$155-$245; and a napkin ring £40-£60/$75-$125, both introduced in 1939, a bowl £50-£80/$95-$165 and two plates. £80-£120/$155-$245 each.

Four Mabel Lucie Attwell plates. In the early versions the faces of the children have very ruddy and generally darker complexions, later the draughtsmanship becomes slicker, more hard-edged, with the children's faces being paler and less ruddy. The elves also generally get tidied up, losing some of their roundness. Top plates £80-£120/$155-$245 each, bottom left £80-£120/$155-$245; bottom right £40-£60/$80-$165.

A part Mabel Lucie Attwell nursery ware tea set (top, £150-£250/$295-$515 part set), two children on a tricycle following a hare. Bottom from left: mug £50-£80/$95-$165; side plate £40-£60/$75-$125; beaker mug £50-£80/$95-$165; with carts of elves and a girl feeding blue birds.

A Mabel Lucie Attwell infant's chamber pot (small), dating from 1934. By 1939 there was also a larger version available for children. £100-£150/£195-$310.

A Shelley Specials Menu. Introduced in 1938 there were a range of designs available including ducks taking to the air, a gaggle of geese, a fashionable young lady walking her two Borzois, as well as a sunburst and tall trees design, amongst others, £200-£400/$390-$820.

'The Golfer' circa 1937, £800-£1000/$1560-$2050.

Two groups of Mabel Lucie Attwell statuettes. Numbers 11, 7, 13 & 14, and below numbers 17, 12 and 10. The colour variation of the statuette second from the right on top, indicates a later date than the others, albeit only ten or fifteen years, not just an individual paintress's variation, as Mabel Lucie Attwell was very conscientious about the quality of production, apparently often making unannounced appearances at the works. £300-£500/$585-$1025 each figure.

A collection of Mabel Lucie Attwell single figures. Circa 1937. 'Toddler', £600-£800/$1170-$1640, 'I's Shy', £700-£900/$1365-$1845 and 'How'm I Doin'', £800-£1000/$1560-$2050. Bottom left: 'The Golfer' £800-£1000/$1560-$2050 and 'Diddlums', £800-£1000/$1560-$2050. Bottom right – the behind of 'Diddlums'.

Three Mabel Lucie Attwell figure groups, circa 1937. Left: 'The Bride' £700-£900/$1365-$1845 and 'The Bridegroom' £700-£900/$1365-$1845; Right: 'Our Pets', £1200-£1600/$2340-$3280.

A part Mabel Lucie Attwell 'Boo-Boo' tea set, circa 1926, £600-£800/$1170-$1640 (£400/$775 in 1994-95. £510/$975 in 1995. £570/$1100 May 1996).

A Mabel Lucie Attwell 'Boo-Boo' Teapot, £250-£350/$490-$715 – together with four Mabel Lucie Attwell statuettes – L.A. 11, L.A.12, L.A.10 and L.A.17 (£300-£500/$585-$1025 each).

The Mabel Lucie Attwell 'Animal Tea set.' Introduced in 1930, by 1934 it was not part of the company's advertising therefore probably not in production, except by special request. £600-£800/$1170-$1640 (£420/$840 for the set in 1995, with chips to the sugar and loss of paint). Bottom: A part tea set with dancing muses on the Vincent shape, circa 1920-30, £150-£250/$295-$515.

No 11628

PATTERN No. 11628
TALL QUEEN ANNE SHAPE

CHINA	£	s	d
Teaset, 21 pieces	2	0	0
,, 40	3	14	6
Coffee Set	1	11	0
Morning Set	1	0	0
Fruit Set	1	6	0
Sandwich Set		16	9
Breakfast Set, 33 pieces	3	5	3
,, 63 ,,	5	18	9
Porridge Plates (semi-porcelain)			
8-in. actual Extra doz.		16	8
SEMI-PORCELAIN			
Dinner Set, 26 pieces	3	3	6
,, 52 ,,	5	19	6
,, 67 ,,	8	8	3
For Scotland			
Dinner Set, 32 pieces	3	3	9
,, 61 ,,	6	14	6
Dessert Set, 9 pcs. (Qn. Anne)	1	2	3
,, 18 ,,	2	4	4
CHINA			
Teapot, approx. 2-pts		12	0
,, ,, 1½ ,,		9	9
,, ,, 1-pt		8	3
Teapot Stand		4	0
COVERED JUG, for hot water or hot milk			
with coffee set (china cover) £ s d			
approx. 2-pts		10	6
,, 1½ ,,		9	3
,, 1-pt		8	0
Extra Cake Plate or Bread and			
Butter Plate, approx. 8-in.			
square		4	0
Open Butter or Jam Dish, 4-in.		1	8
,, ,, 5 ,,		2	6
Cov. Preserve (1) 2½-in. high		3	0
,, (2) 2¾ ,,		4	0
,, (3) 3½ ,,		5	0
Covered Muffin (8-in. diam.)		10	6

For composition of sets see inside front
cover.

WE WILL TAKE COFFEE IN THE
DRAWING ROOM . . .

AND AS HOSTESS YOU WILL EX
CUSE THE ENVY IN THE EYES OF
YOUR GUESTS WHEN THEY SEE THE
SHELLEY SET YOU HAVE CHOSEN,
THEN WITH WHAT PRIDE AND
HOW DAINTILY YOU WILL SIP FROM
YOUR OWN FRAGRANT CUP.

Sales brochure dating from about 1930 showing the Tall Queen Anne Shape.

92

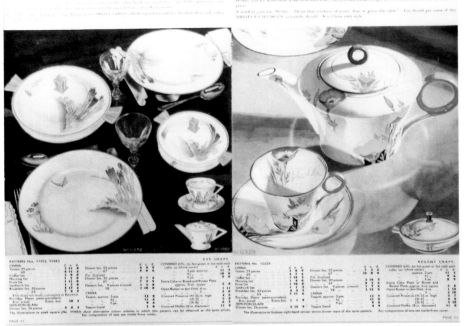

Last page of a Shelley sales brochure dating, circa 1930, (Top) showing Mabel Lucie Attwell Nursery Ware, the 'Boo-Boo' tea set and 'Dainty White' china. Bottom - Retailers brochure, dating from circa 1933-35, showing the Eve and Regent shapes.

Further pages from the same retailer's brochure, circa 1933-35, showing Polkadot on Regent, Bands and Lines on Eve and below Silk (also known as Pyjama Stripe) and Phlox flowers both on Regent. Notice the various colourways.

One that Got Away. Every so often odd pieces escape from all the potteries and Shelley is no exception as seen here with this rather decorative meat plate. This is what might be called a 'sampler piece', showing as many of the then current transfers in use. I was shown this plate by a former worker several years ago but can you spot the date it was made-up?

Top left: an Avon shaped plate with 'Aegean' £10-£20/$19-$40; and below a part Avon shape coffee set, 1964 to 1966, decorated with the 'Apollo' design (£30-£40/$55-$80), both designs registered on 1st December 1964. Top right is a rare commemorative bowl for the Coronation of Queen Elizabeth II, 1953, decorated with raised turquoise enamel lettering on a broad gilt band, £80-£120/$155-$245.

Guide to Illustrations

This section, hopefully, is self-explanatory. What follows is intended to be a helpful and understandable guide to some of the shapes, patterns and types of ware used to illustrate this book. The illustrations have been chosen to represent some highlights of typical Shelley production, any attempt to try and cover all aspects of Shelley production would unfortunately have taken up more pages than the format of this book allows.

You will find in the following pages that a fair amount of time in spent talking about the tea ware trios, rather than the figures. This is mainly because the figures do not need much explanation and neither, for that matter, does much of the Frederick Rhead and Walter Slater art pottery. If there is no mention of crested and heraldic china, jelly, commemorative wares and a few other types, then that is because they have been mentioned elsewhere or because I have tended to deal with the more populist wares. In other areas there are, of course, other specialist books, chintz being one such an example.

Just to be slightly controversial for a moment, if I might be so bold, and speaking with a design historians hat on, there are certain patterns or styles of surface pattern that are totally inappropriate for ceramic wares, however populist they were at the time and might have since become. There is a necessary balance and harmony needed between the surface decoration of an object and the shape, without which the object can start to look ugly. At its most extreme, the complete lack of consideration between object and decoration leaves a totally undesirable result, verging on the 'kitsch.' It's all very well being influenced by something or a collection of things, styles, colours and/or patterns from which one then creates a new response or look, the result of which shows consideration of the shape and size of the surface the decoration is intended for. Just to take a pattern from another object, such as a length of fabric or a curtain, and apply it, without any further thought, care or consideration, onto an object for which the pattern had never been intended, either in scale, use, texture or lighting, is I would suggest the height of ineptitude. It also smacks in the face of the consumer who, largely, has to rely on the available market choice from which to make their selection.

Whilst the vast majority of Shelley collectors only have eyes for the china tea and dinner wares there are equally collectable, sometimes even more expensive, earthenwares produced at the Shelley pottery. The wares I am specifically talking about are commonly known as Intarsio wares, although this generalized term also includes some variations as we shall see. These wares form the first twenty-five or so colour illustrations in this book and although these wares have been mentioned earlier it is worth making a few comments regarding the actual illustrations.

What has been illustrated in this section, as is probably apparent, are almost all from the 'Intarsio' range of wares created and designed by Frederick Rhead, sometime between 1897 and 1905. They were very popular at the time and were accordingly made in large numbers, a high proportion of which have survived. Of the information that survives in the archive and elsewhere, it would appear that pattern number 3001 is the first of the Intarsio wares, dating from about 1897, and the numbers seem to go beyond 7600 under the directorship of Walter Slater in 1909. Not all of these patterns are Intarsio and there are large gaps in between, for example, there are no 5000 numbers. The pattern books are by no means complete which does not help, however, by the time Frederick Rhead left, sometime in 1905, the numbers has reached circa pattern number 7296.

As can be seen from the captions the prices vary considerably, due in part to visual appearance, size and personal tastes but also rarity. An example of this (not illustrated) is the model of a seated cat, looking to the right with wide eyes and pointed ears. This feline model, 9½ inches (24cm) high, was decorated with several patterns and colours, fleur-de-lys being a typical design which sells for between £400-£600/$780-$1230. The same model decorated with leaping and running mice can be worth between £2000-£3000/$3900-$6150 in perfect condition.

The illustrations on page 11 and page 33 show that Intarsio wares were made as large as umbrella stands, stick stands and as a jardiniere and stand. Some of these wares formed part of the innovative early promotion schemes, that were later in the 1920s and 1930s to be more comprehensively applied. Large hall umbrella stands, as illustrated on page 31, were decorated with the words 'The Foley China' and 'For our customers' use', such stands being distributed to retailers as promotional advertising. In the same vein small rectangular plaques, with 'Depot for The Foley China, England's Finest Porcelain', were made for inclusion in window displays to attract passing custom. The most well-known promotional piece from the Shelley pottery being the model of the 'Shelley Girl', seated on a column holding a cup in her hand (illustration page 14).

Tea Ware Trios
Colour pictures on page 59
This page shows one of the early, highly recognizable, shape designs Alexandra that was registered November 1886 (No: 60650) and used until about 1902. This is a very common shape, having been sold with somewhere in the region of 162 patterns. The top two patterns, both monochrome transfer prints, display a Japanese influence, prevalent in European design from the mid 1860s, part of the design, being interrupted by a completely different pattern and at the same time disappearing over the edge of the shape. The middle left illustration is what many will be more familiar with in terms of the Japanese influence, namely the 'Imari' palette, named after a certain type of decoration which involved the use of the colours red, blue and gilt, the blue usually being underglaze. This particular shape must have been highly uncomfortable to drink out of, having such a scalloped edge, not to mention the overall quatrelobed form. The visual effect created by the shape is one of a very light delicate almost lace-like quality. The bottom two designs display a slightly more subdued and subtle pattern, as opposed to the completely covered and rather heavy design of the above.

The bottom right design Lily, introduced in 1888 and still in the pattern books in 1918, is an altogether more simple, plain and functional shape. Functional in that the narrow width of the mouth kept the liquid contents warmer for far longer than the Alexandra shapes.

Colour pictures on page 60
Top left is another Lily shape but with a rather odd monochrome transfer printed pattern which seems to have been either badly cut up and placed or a deliberate combination of two, if not three, different designs. Top and middle right is the Daisy shape, registered in the same year Lily was introduced, 1888 and was last recorded in the pattern books in 1913. 1913 was a natural cut off year for many designs as a consequence of the first world war. This has a distinctive up pointing handle and lobed body, also reflected in the cloud-like plates and saucers. A year later a more simplified design than that of Daisy emerged, namely Fairy which was in use for five years, from 1890 to 1895, during which time it bore some 216 pattern designs, two of which can be seen on the bottom left and right. This shape design also retains the upwardly pointing handle design. There remains one further illustration

on this page, middle left. This shape looks very like the Daisy design next to it on the right, the cup size and height are the same, the overall lobed form is the same, the saucers are identical and the plate designs, although not the same size, are the same. Even the angle and shape of the handle are the same. In fact, you might have thought they were the same, had I not been writing in this manner. The one major difference is that the left-hand cup has a twist in the body towards the base. Unfortunately, none of the pattern books or published books I have seen seems to indicate a name or date for this piece. Just to confuse matters further, a new version of this cup was designed in 1899 called Violet, illustrated on page 64 which has a very slightly deeper cup. Such small differences can make all the difference when trying to build up a collection of this type, especially when so many shapes where altered or added to later in their lives.

In terms of surface pattern, it is interesting to see a slightly lighter aspect to these patterns, the designs again all being executed using transfer prints, with the exception of the middle right which has additional colour handpainted filling in the printed outline. On the reverse of the previous page (middle left), just a quick note about the bottom two that you've probably already noticed, the border transfers are the same on the plates and cups, although using different colours, but the trio on the right has additional star-motif and flower transfers in the centers.

Colour pictures on page 61

Daisy continues from the previous page, top left, this time returning to the completely covered Japanese influenced designs we saw on the Alexandra ware at the beginning. Although it has not been mentioned yet, it's worthwhile noting that every piece illustrated so far, indeed many of those to follow, have gilt-banded edges and often gilt-detailing to the handles. This is significant in that it indicates the type of consumer to whom the Wileman pottery would have been marketing their wares, namely the middle and upper middle classes. As we shall see later the practice of gilt banding edging was much diminished just prior the First World War.

The remaining illustrations of this page, with the exception of the bottom left, are all in the Empire shape, introduced in 1893 and still in the pattern books in 1910. The two illustrations, top right and middle left show how two very similar patterns can look after one has been additionally hand coloured. At the bottom left is a very exotic, if not somewhat over embellished, shape called, unsurprisingly, Shell. Used between 1891 and 1894, there would appear to have been some 86 patterns used on this shape, a great many pieces no doubt finding their way into various display cabinets. This trio also exhibits the rather incongruous application of a transfer print on heavily moulded pieces, something of which many of the potteries during turn of the nineteenth century were all to often guilty. In this case, the design does make an effort to sympathize with the very undulating form. But then consideration for and some empathy towards the all-important relationship between shape and pattern was always something pursued by those associated with design at the Wileman and (later) Shelley works.

Colour pictures on page 62

Carrying on the theme from the previous page the top two and middle left shapes are again in the Empire design, with the top two showing different colour-ways of the same pattern. The middle left design shows a very heavy use of the Japanese 'Imari' influence, used by numerous potteries in Britain but perhaps most notably by the Royal Crown Derby factory. One thing that can be clearly seen in this illustration are the sequences involved in the process of decoration, namely the broad, somewhat crude for Wileman, underglaze handpainted cobalt-blue background, over which the red transfer print has then been applied, before the final gilt, handpainted in this case, has been applied. Although having said that you may notice that the side plate of this trio does not have any gilt. This is either because it never had any when it escaped from the factory or and more likely it has worn, even perhaps been deliberately worn, away. (For the latter, see the chapter on restoration.)

Another new shape is Century seen in the right middle and bottom left. This was introduced in 1895 and lasted until about 1902, during which time it hosted 122 patterns. This particular shape design is quite simple and useable, certainly when compared to some of the others. It seems to warrant the use of light, subtle patterns that can compliment the shape. A point of interest here the bottom two trios is not only that both have the same basic printed pattern but also the use of a graduated two-tone colour transfer print.

The shape on the bottom left is perhaps the most famous of the pottery's shapes, without a doubt the longest in production, namely Dainty. Looking at Century and then at Dainty an almost natural progression in the shape design can be seen.

Colour pictures on page 63
Registered in 1896, the Dainty shape was still in production some seventy years later, in 1966, when the factory was taken over. The shape was designed by Rowland Morris and throughout its history had an ever increasing and fluctuating number of pieces in the range. There were two versions, low and tall, and in 1932 there was also the addition of a floral handle. It can clearly be seen why the shape become so popular, having the strong lobed basic form seen in previous designs, combined with the delicate fine fluted fan-shaped panels around the border. The odd addition of the floral handle was something a few potteries were prone to incorporating at the time and is more a fashion statement then anything else. The normal handle is very useable and the cups perform their task well. This was an important consideration, as the buying public started to become slightly more discerning, even more so the highly critical American consumers. Word must soon have spread in the United States that not only was this new shape particularly fine but that it also fulfilled the basic requirement of a tea set. The Dainty shape was an extremely good seller in the United States, which was largely responsible for the longevity of the design. The American market was further responsible for the high volume of dinner ware sets that were sold, something that developed during the beginning of the twentieth century and still further during the later years of the Shelley production. Some of the typically distinctive features associated with the Dainty shape that can be seen illustrated here are the use of monochrome and two-tone colours and the use of the classic scattered 'Elizabethan Rose' pattern, although here as a variant with other flowers amongst the roses.

Even though there were probably somewhere in the region of five hundred plus patterns, not including commemorative wares, used on Dainty, partly due to its longevity, the most popular seller was 'Dainty White', that is just plain white. Dainty became so popular that it had its own advertising brochure if to detail the wide range of wares were available; far to many to mention here. One of the most bizarre shapes has to be a scallop shaped tray with recesses for a tea set for four. It is also worth looking out for miniature white pieces. Before leaving the Dainty shape, it is worth noting that you two registration numbers that belong to this shape can be found.

At the bottom right on this page is another design introduced in the same year as Dainty, namely Snowdrop. Here the Snowdrop shape is decorated with a light colourful transfer print, a pattern which has room to breathe.

Colour pictures on page 64

If there is one thing that the Snowdrop shape was influenced by, it was the prevalent style of the period, Art Nouveau. Here, in the top two illustrations as well as the middle left, the sweeping curves of the body are reflected in the two highly stylized floral patterns, so typical of this new decorative scheme. Introduced in 1896 Snowdrop was used until 1914. With such a strong and bold shape numerous patterns seem well suited to it, from the bold and all consuming Japanese 'Imari' style design, in red, blue and gilt, as seen in the middle right trio to the more reserved, again 'Imari' influenced design at the bottom left. This design highlights the broad hand painted underglaze cobalt blue blocks of colour, contrasted with the high detail of the red coloured applied transfer print.

Three years later, in 1899, Violet was introduced, seen on the bottom right. Although this shape seems to owe a great deal in terms of style to Snowdrop, Violet was introduced as an alternative to the Fairy shape seen on page 60. This version having a deeper cup. All three shapes have lobed bodies and pointed handles. Snowdrop, however, has that extra deluxe kink in the body, allowing for the fuller swelling of the mouth, not to mention the addition of the small foot-ring which in turn allows the vertical swelling lobes have rounded ends.

Colour pictures on page 65

Top left is another Violet shape trio, as seen on the previous page, transfer printed with repeated pendant flowers and foliage from scrolling acanthus on the rim. This is followed, top right and middle left, by two transfer printed patterns, this time of overlapping floral swags, in two colour-ways on the Court shape. This shape first appears in the pattern books in 1906, although it was registered in 1904, and was in production until 1913.

Leaving the pre-war period, indeed the Wileman period behind, the illustrations leap ahead to the post war period of 1916, six years after the pottery began trading under the name Shelley China, when the Vincent shape was introduced. This shape was to hold a vast number of patterns, over 200, until 1933, due to its clean lines and flat cylindrical sides (another example is seen bottom left). If examined more closely there is also a noticeable change in appearance from all the preceding illustrations. In fact there are a few changes but the most noticeable is the lack of any gilt on the rims. Other changes from the pre-war designs of all the previous pages are the use of a landscape as the design, something that was to become highly popular in the following two decades. Another interesting feature seen on the landscape design is the use of heavy on glaze enamel decoration over the colour washed ground and the transfer printed pattern. The bottom left Vincent shape also displays the new use of a bold lithographic design using flat blocks of colour.

Finally, the portents of things to come with perhaps the most desirable, in terms of the most widely sought after, shape that Shelley made, Queen Anne. This particular pattern 'My Garden' (No: 11607) introduced in 1928, is a development of the pattern above on the Vincent shape, both employing transfer prints which have then been enameled on the surface.

Colour pictures on page 66

The next two pages are devoted to the Queen Anne shape, with more illustrations on other pages. If nothing else this indicates how prolific and popular this shape was, selling to many countries around the world. Introduced in August 1926 the Queen Anne shape was a development of previous octagonal shape designs, the first being Square, registered in 1884, which was also often referred to as Queen Anne. Later came Antique, 1905 to 1914, with its version of the octagonal shape tapering to the base and applied with a sharp pointed handle.

That the Antique shape formed the basis for the Queen Anne shape, although it had not been produced for twelve years, can be seen by the occurence of several shapes, sugar bowls and some milk jugs, in the Queen Anne range that are identical to those used in the Antique designs.

Looking at some of the illustrations on pages 65 and 66 what becomes noticeable in the contrasting designs that were used on the shape. Some of the designs are still relatively conservative with small motifs, printed as well as printed and enameled, often based on classical imagery. Many designs, such as Blue Iris (bottom left) made good use of the simple shape, showing off the minimalist motifs to best effect. These sympathetic designs jar sharply with the introduction, in 1928, of various designs based on cottages in landscapes. Although these designs were to prove highly popular, selling very well right into the early 1930s, the total disregard for the paneled effects of the octagonal shape leaves a great deal wanting.

Colour pictures on page 67

The above point is illustrated by the second page devoted to the Queen Anne shape. The top two illustrations, 'Cottage – 2', introduced in September 1928, illustrate the wonderfully languid, dreamily idyllic, rural haven to which the viewer might aspire, yet the design rambles across the carefully considered moulded shape as if it was not there. The height of the failure, in terms of 'good design' and harmony between shape and pattern, is best seen on the cup where the design is fighting a losing battle with the form. Such was the popularity of this design that it was even available with gold edging, something once standard that was rarely seen in the 1920s. The next design, only three patterns later, is a very striking, boldly coloured stylized rendition of stick-thin tall trees, borrowed from 'Cottage – 1', holding circular fruits with birds in flight in the distance. This design has been given the name 'Balloon Tree' and was altogether more successful in terms of design, the pattern being more thoughtfully drawn so that it could be adapted for a greater variety of shapes.

It should be pointed out at this stage that very, very few designs, considering the thousands that were used, were actually given pattern names by the factory. Only subsequently, usually for collectors to distinguish one pattern from another or for ease of understanding, have names became associated with certain patterns, therefore 'Balloon Trees' is at once understood because of the multicoloured balloon shaped fruits on the tree. The next design however, Crabtree, was given its name at the pottery. It is also interesting for another reason, namely that the decoration was applied using a coloured lithographic print, not something new to the potteries but something more associated with the cheaper unskilled wares of minor potteries. The only remaining hand painting on this design is the edging.

Undoubtedly one of the most successful designs, judging by the number of set, part sets and remaining pieces, was 'Sunset and Tall Trees.' This pattern was still being advertised in the late 1930s, long after its contemporaries had vanished and one can quite see why. Promoted as "Brightness in the Home" the Sunset pattern, as it was often called, sold well abroad as well as in Britain but perhaps this was because it was available, for the first time, with an earthenware dinner service, promoted as 'semi-porcelain' (see illustration page 92). Previous such dinner sets were only available in china and even then generally seem to have been used mainly for display. The last design on this page 'Anemone', introduced in October 1932, shows an altogether lighter and more open use of pattern compared to the previous designs, yet unfortunately is just as unsympathetic when it comes to considering the form onto which the design was to go.

I might seem a little ingenious here, expecting every design to conform totally and fit like a tailor-made suit or dress, but then knowing something of the working processes of a commercial pottery, it is true to say that new shape designs once developed, generated new pattern designs that would suit. Only all to often these two aspects of the design process, shape design and pattern design, would be worked on by different, and often none communicating, departments. What happens after a new shape is generated is that new patterns are then developed on paper, often following or filling in a template of the new shape. The immediate problem here is that by designing on paper some of designers appear not to have been thinking in the round, also the template would be fine for a plate, but when it came to other parts of the ware, such as a cup or bowl quite often, not always, the designs would not suit. I suspect that much of the problem also lay with the concept of throwing to many designs onto a new shape, in the hope of appealing to as wide a number of customers as possible.

Colour pictures on page 68

The top two illustrations on this page really test the nerves when it comes to identifying and dating. Looking at the pattern on the top left, you would be forgiven for thinking that it dates from about 1916-17 when the Cloisonné pattern, number 8321, on black was introduced and that as a consequence the shape must be the Antique shape of a few years previously. You would be right about the pattern, but wrong about the shape and date. The shape is Queen Anne, notice the curved corners of the saucer and the plate, the Antique having straight edges, and therefore the date is between 1926 and 1933. These two patterns are in fact to be found in the Seconds pattern books, usually reserved for an inferior body, utilizing cheaper designs with no or little additional painting to the print.

The next four illustrations are what might be called dramatically different. This was very much the height of fashion and as such did not stay around for long, something that the management at Shelleys were aware of. The two shapes in question are Vogue, middle left, and Mode, middle right, both introduced in 1930, Vogue was the first to make it to the pattern books in August, one month before Mode. When these two designs were released onto the market, they caused quite a stir, the reaction was initially somewhat subdued but then more generously praised. The severe angularity of the shape together with the highly geometric style of the patterns completely broke with tradition, something many critics of the industry, which had previously been more prone to the safety of the tried and tested traditional designs, had advocated for some time. Such daringly bold shapes take a great deal of imagination and skill to conceive and are obviously the result of contemporary influences from Europe which would have included Cubism and Art Deco. It was, however, the confidence of Eric Slater that achieved the end result. Numerous British companies took up this style in a wide variety of media, from the novelty end right the way through. A populist pattern that has come to typify the style of this period and one which crossed many media boundaries is the Sunray motif. This could, indeed still can, be found on garden gates, garage doors, front doors, domestic stained glass windows, speaker covers of wirelesses (radios today) and carpet designs, not to mention forming the background to advertising material and a whole host of other graphic material. Shelleys were no exception, as they came up with a quite spectacular and extremely popular design, Sunray (No: 11742) as the second main pattern to be designed for the Vogue shape in 1930 (see page 72).

On this page there are three colour variations of the what has become known as the Blocks pattern, introduced sometime in early 1931, each on the Vogue shape. The Mode shape has another variation of the design which had five colour-ways. Note that the way to spot the difference between the two shapes is that the Vogue shape is smaller but much wider, with a narrow angular foot, while Mode is altogether more upright, the body tapering only slightly by comparison, with hardly any foot to speak of. Both have the instantly recognizable and highly innovative filled-in triangular handles. Innovative, perhaps, but not very practical. Try holding a cup full of tea for any length of time with anything less than perfectly dry fingers and you will see what I mean. Thankfully, the teapot had a pierced handle!

Colour pictures on page 69

Part of the success of these two ranges, Vogue (top right) and Mode (top left), although less often talked about, was the harmony that was achieved between the shape and the specifically designed patterns. The angularity of the shapes demanded angularity and/or abstraction of the image and the latter can be seen to good effect on the next page, with the highly stylized butterfly wing design. This pattern was introduced sometime in 1930 and appears in at least three different colour-ways, one of which is a rare special order for the retailer Plummer, printed in Mauve and pink rather than black and yellow. Even the handle on this design is given special treatment. The Vogue shape in the top right shows the second pattern to be used on this shape, commonly known as 'J', the stylized geometric design that was the trademark of this fashionable ware. Below is another illustration along similar lines. To the left of this is a new shape, as are the remaining two illustrations, which was probably introduced as a consequence of criticism attached to the practicality, or rather lack of it, of the solid triangular handles of the Vogue and Mode shapes. Whatever the reason, Eve was launched in March 1932 as a combination very much of the previous two shape designs. Eve was neither as wide as Vogue, which allows the tea to cool quite rapidly, nor as narrow as Mode, yet had the more gentle tapering effect to the body. It was raised on a foot very much akin to that of Vogue but had the all-important new pierced or open triangular handle. Designs applied to the Eve shape were mostly those used on Vogue and Mode, however, Queen Anne designs also appeared, in an effort to generate some of the phenomenal interest associated with that design. As with Queen Anne, Eve tea ware designs were also offered with a matching dinnerware set, which probably helped sales. In this illustration we can see the rather more conservative use of the Daisies pattern, introduced in 1932, with its pastel colours.

On the bottom left we can see a clear change of direction from Eric Slater with the introduction of the Regent shape in September 1932, just as the Vogue shape was coming to an end and Mode having already been replaced by Eve. The angularity of the previous three shapes has disappeared. Instead it was the mixture of curves and circles that interested Eric Slater. The flared trumpet-shaped body was reflected in all the pieces, even in the design of the saucer. Many of the patterns used on this shape were newly designed floral motifs, often with one predominant bold colour painted over a printed design. Somewhat strangely many of the patterns specifically designed for Vogue, Mode and Eve were also used, with most, especially the highly geometric designs, sitting uncomfortably on such curvilinear shapes. The illustrated pattern, Phlox, introduced shortly after the shape, is more typical of the patterns used on Regent. The fact that this shape was in continuous production until 1940, making use of over 220 patterns, is a testament to the popularity and success of the design. More sporadic uses of the shape can also be found into the 1950s.

At the bottom right is the Oxford shape. Introduced in 1934, this design ran concurrently with Regent, lasting until 1939, and was specifically developed to be used for coffee. Comparing the two shapes side by side, the similarities are quite apparent, Oxford merely having a taller more curvaceous body with an ovoid handle. The patterns used were therefore almost identical to those of the Regent shape.

Colour pictures on page 70

The top four designs here are in the Henley shape which was a new design in August 1938 and had all but disappeared by 1940. It has a slightly waisted body with the now familiar angular small foot. The jointed partial circle handle continues from Lomond and Empire. The patterns during this period often seem to have matching coloured handle, foot and edging and the floral designs became far crisper in draughtsmanship and use of bold colouring, particularly in the top two. This was a trait of the technique of the decoration, namely lithography. The middle left shows the ever present saleability of the 'Elizabethan Rose' style design, based on an image of small rose bud surrounded by leaves, scattered loosely on the surface. Popular since before 1900, the design spawned many variations, of which this is one. Beside this on the middle right is the opposite concept showing the use of another lithographic design completely covering the surface of ware with bunches of flowers on a coloured ground.

The final trio Perth, was introduced either to replace Regent, as it was originally called New Regent, or as an alternative to harmonize with Henley. The former seems more likely, especially when you compare the basic body outline which is basically the same, with the addition of a double clipped rim and a different handle. The effect of the shape combined with the patterns, particularly the one illustrated, marks a return to the more sober, conservative and safe levels of the greater buying public that Shelley so much depended upon. This shape however had rather a short life. Introduced in about December 1939 and last entering the pattern books in January 1940, by which time it had only adopted nine patterns. However, like so many of the shapes and patterns things are never that straightforward, designs being used on later shapes years after they were supposedly axed and the same with some of the shape designs. When there are fifty or sixty thousand transfers lying about in a storeroom, they might occasionally get used later on.

Nursery Wares

The production of Nursery wares is something that many potteries venture into from time to time and Shelleys were no different. The great interest in Nursery wares developed at about the turn of the century, and the earliest known nursery wares produced at Shelley appear to date from circa 1896. This series consisted of six designs of a boy and girl or two girls in various scenes with farm animals or wildlife. In 1902, another series was registered, this time comprising nursery rhymes such as 'The Three Bears', 'Red Riding Hood' and 'Babes in the Wood'.

The earliest wares were often of a high moral tone depicting teenage children with appropriate verse and captions such as 'Be Prepared', 'Conscience'. Children were shown in naturalistic scenes, or at least in scenes or at activities which their parents would hope to have been normal. The images were more often than not to please the parents and not the children. Most of the early nursery ware designs were either bought in from anonymous artists or largely taken from known illustrations. One such set of designs was 'Puff-Puff' dating from about 1910, depicting a six or so trains and another, dating from 1914, depicted naval scenes.

Some of the most individual designs were created by Hilda Cowham and Mabel Lucie Attwell during the 1920s and through the 1930s. There is even some suggestion that the Animal Series, 1917, of dogs, cockerels and a hen, might have been commissioned from Hilda Cowham, but that would seem a little premature. In the Specials pattern book there is a design for a covered box called the 'Cowham Box', dated between September 1926 and January 1927. This depicts a girl kneeling on a cushion holding a bouquet of flowers in her right hand, represented in two different colourways.

Early Nursery Ware – Most of the following had a series of six different designs.

	Baby Plate	Mug/C&S	Bowl	Side plate
Puff-Puff – circa 1910	£20-£30/ $39-$60	£20-£30/ $39-$60	£10-£15/ $19-$30	£10-£15/ $19-$30
Peter Pan – circa 1910	£20-£30/ $39-$60	£20-£30/ $39-$60	£10-£15/ $19-$30	£10-£15/ $19-$30
New Nursery – 1913	£20-£30/ $39-$60	£20-£30/ $39-$60	£10-£15/ $19-$30	£10-£15/ $19-$30
Naval Scenes – 1914	£20-£30/ $39-$60	£20-£30/ $39-$60	£10-£15/ $19-$30	£10-£15/ $19-$30
Children at play – circa 1914	£20-£30/ $39-$60	£20-£30/ $39-$60	£10-£15/ $19-$30	£10-£15/ $19-$30
Ride a Cock Horse – 1916	£20-£30/ $39-$60	£20-£30/ $39-$60	£10-£15/ $19-$30	£10-£15/ $19-$30
Animal Series – 1917	£20-£30/ $39-$60	£20-£30/ $39-$60	£10-£15/ $19-$30	£10-£15/ $19-$30
Bryta Nursery Ware –1918	£20-£30/ $39-$60	£20-£30/ $39-$60	£10-£15/ $19-$30	£10-£15/ $19-$30
Dutch Children – 1923	£20-£30/ $39-$60	£20-£30/ $39-$60	£10-£15/ $19-$30	£10-£15/ $19-$30

Linda Edgerton Rhymes 1924/5	£20-£30/ $39-$60	£20-£30/ $39-$60	£10-£15/ $19-$30	£10-£15/ $19-$30
Hilda Cowham Nursery Rhyme & Fairyland – 1925	£30-£40/ $55-$80	£30-£40/ $55-$80	£20-£30/ $39-$60	£20-£30/ $39-$60
'Playtime' –-1927	£30-£40/ $55-$80	£30-£40/ $55-$80	£20-£30/ $39-$60	£20-£30/ $39-$60

Nursery Ware Tea set

Tent Teapot	£500-£600/$975-$1230
Shell Milk Jug	£250-£350/$490-$715
Sugar bucket	£250-£350/$490-$715

Nursery Ware tea set, 1928, which had a wonderfully modelled tent shaped teapot with two children reading a comic inside, a sugar bowl in the form of a bucket and a shell moulded milk jug with a mermaid sitting on a rock painted on the side. In 1995 a complete set with a restored lid sold for £840/$1600 whereas today such a set would be worth between £1000-£1500/$1950-$3075.

Mabel Lucie Attwell
Animals & Children – 1926
This Animals and Children set, often called 'Boo-Boo' nursery ware depicts little elves in green clothes, continued in production into the 1950s with pieces being added and withdrawn to the set over the years. Initially there were six plate designs registered in June 1926. The most innovative and talked about pieces, namely the mushroom-modelled tea set, with the highly characteristic 'Boo-Boo' milk jug quickly followed the printed ware.

In 1934 promotional leaflets indicate that there were something like sixteen different pieces of china and eleven pieces of semi-porcelain that could be bought. By 1939 there were twenty-three china shapes and twenty-three semi-porcelain pieces available. The price list for the china wares gives a sample of prices indicating what other pieces might be (see list).

Boo-Boo tea set – semi-porcelain

Teapot 1½ (1926)	£300-£400/$585-$820
Milk (Boo-Boo)	£150-£200/$295-$410
Sugar	£150-£200/$296-$410
Cruet (circa1930)	£120-£180/$235-$370
Infant's Chamber pot	£100-£150/$195-$305
Baby Plate, round	£80-£120/$155-$245
Baby Plate, oval	£80-£120/$155-$245
Baby Plate, sm. round	£40-£60/$75-$125
Porridge Plate	£40-£60/$75-$125
Deep oatmeal saucer	£30-£50/$55-$100
Teapot (1 pint)	£120-£180/$235-$370
Meat Plate (1937)	£80-£120/$155-$245
Fruit Saucer (stone rim)	£40-£60/$75-$125
Pudding Plate 9"	£40-£60/$75-$125
Pudding Plate 8"	£30-£50/$55-$100
Covered Hot Plate	£80-£120/$155-$245
Hot Water Plate(no Cover)	£50-£80/$95-$165

Serviette Ring	£40-£60/$75-$125
Milk jug (mushroom)	£80-£120/$155-$245
Covered Jug (1½ pint)	£50-£80/$95-$165
Covered Jug (1 pint)	£40-£60/$75-$125
Child's Chamber (large)	£70-£90/$135-$185
Orange Squeezer	
(decorated as sugar)	£50-£80/$95-$165
Electric Night Lamp (1936)	£200-£300/$390-$715

The Electric night lamp, sometimes known as 'Sleepy-head', came boxed "with a 15 watt miniature bulb, 3 yards of art silk flex and a two pin plug/lampholder adapter, making an ideal gift". This could also be supplied in special colours to order. There were also standard table lamps available, at least four or five, onto which any of the nursery ware transfer prints could be put, the shade being hand painted with 'Gnomes', as they were called in the brochures. What is equally revealing in studying the brochures is that the 'Boo-Boo' tea set is the only nursery ware set being promoted after 1934, which may explain the relative rarity of the Mabel Lucie Attwell 'Animal' set and the Hilda Cowham 'Playtime' tea set.

1936 saw the introduction of a variety of table lamps, with matching shades, with various permutations in terms of size and decoration. In the 1937 retailers' catalogue there are lamps called 'Virgo' and 'Orion' which could be supplied in four sizes and with various different coloured grounds, each with the 'highest quality Velinoid' shades, decorated to match. Also available were two china lamp bases, both nameless, with matching china shades, one with the body and shade in the form of a bell and the other a faceted sphere with a bell shaped shade. Other shapes included; 'Neptune', 'Mercury', 'Saturn', 'Pluto', 'Vega', 'Spica', 'Petral', 'Uranus' and 'Jupiter', each with 'Velinoid' shades.

Aside from these you could also order any of the 'single' figures and the double figure, 'Our Pets', to be put onto a base with a 9 or 11 inch diameter pink, blue, green or orange Velinoid shade. It would also appear that the figures could be "supplied in special colours to order".

Mabel Lucie Attwell
Animal tea wares set, modelled in 1930, this can be seen on page 91 with a Duck teapot, Rabbit milk jug and Chicken sugar bowl. In 1995 such a set was selling for circa £500/$975 for the set in 1995 and today would realise £1000-£1500/$1950-$3075.

Gnomes Figures – 1937
Variable; 6½cm to 7½cm high

		Figure
Skipping/Dancing	No: 7	£300-£500/$585-$1025
Jockey	No: 10	£300-£500/$585-$1025
Pixie with Mushroom	No: 11	£300-£500/$585-$1025
Riding a Smiling Dog	No: 12	£300-£500/$585-$1025
Traveller	No: 13	£300-£500/$585-$1025
Thirsty	No: 14	£300-£500/$585-$1025
Gardener	No: 17	£300-£500/$585-$1025
Mushroom Village (1940s)	—	£300-£500/$585-$1025
Little Mermaid (1940s)	—	£300-£500/$585-$1025
Pixie with Mushroom (1940s)	LA23	£300-£500/$585-$1025
(possible re-issue of No: 11)		

Riding a Smiling Dog (1940s) (possible re-issue of No: 12)	LA24	£300-£500/$585-$1025
Jockey (possible re-issue of No: 10)	LA26	£300-£500/$585-$1025 (£310/$600 – 1995)
Riding a Rabbit (1940s)	—	£300-£500/$585-$1025
Riding a Duck with Reins (1940s)	—	£300-£500/$585-$1025
Winged Pixie on a Mushroom	LA33	£300-£500/$585-$1025

Single Figures – 1937
Invariably 15cm high.

		Figure
The Toddler	LA1	£600-£800/$1170-$1640
The Toddler	LA2	£600-£800/$1170-$1640 (£780/$1600 – 1999)
The Toddler	LA3	£600-£800/$1170-$1640
The Curate	LA4	£800-£1000/$1560-$2050 (£340/$640 – 1992)
The Bride	LA5	£700-£900/$1365-$1845
The Bridegroom	LA6	£700-£900/$1365-$1845
The Golfer	LA8	£800-£1000/$1560-$2050 (£420/$795 – 1992)
I's Shy	LA9	£700-£900/$1365-$1845 (£240/$450 – 1992; £670/$1295 – 1995)
Diddlums	LA15	£800-£1000/$1560-$2050 (£340/$640 – 1992)
How'm I Doin'	LA16	£800-£1000/$1560-$2050 (£340/$640 – 1992)
I's Goin Tata	LA18	£1200-£1600/$2340-$3280 (£1550/$3175 – 1999)
Our Pets	LA19	£1200-£1600/$2340-$3280
Gardener's Boy (1950)	LA22	£800-£1000/$1560-$2050

In July 1992 Sotheby's Sussex salerooms sold 'The Curate', 'How'm I Doin' ', 'The Golfer', 'I's Shy" and 'Diddlums', all the lots going for between £240/$450 (hammer) for 'I's Shy' to £420/$795 (hammer) for 'The Golfer'. Nothing unusual you might say except that each model had a special wooden stand, a name card and its original green box. Surely today, such a single figure with everything mentioned above must be worth between £1800-£2000/$3510-$4100.

It has been reported that Shelley Nursery ware even has a Royal connection, with the former two Royal Princesses, Elizabeth and Margaret Windsor, each having a Mabel Lucie Attwell designed nursery ware set, and later Prince Charles having his own version as well!

Shortly after the war, whilst the new 'Mushroom Village' and 'Little Mermaid' were selling well, the 'Boo-Boo' china nursery tablewares were falling out of favour. The only way that Shelleys could continue to produce the wares was to share the costs of the lithographs that were becoming expensive. In 1956 permission was given by Mabel Lucie Attwell's agents for Shelley and the firm of Simpsons, Cobridge, to both use the 'Boo-Boo' lithographs, Simpsons were to use them on earthenware so that Shelley could continue produce their bona china versions.

The later re-issues of the Pixie with Mushroom and Riding a Smiling Dog involve a repositioning of heads and limbs more then anything else, but of course, they also appear, as with all the later statuettes in stronger brighter colours. It would seem that there might be more Mabel Lucie Attwell single figures, as well as miniatures, out there. (But don't forget there are also some very good fakes out there as well, as mentioned in another chapter.)

Restoration

Repairs, Damage and Faults

This chapter is as much about factory faults as it is about restoration. Not that the two things are in any way related, in fact far from it. Restoration is the deliberate attempt, through the action of a human hand, to cover up damage, defect or blemish, whereas a factory fault is something that occurs to a piece during manufacture or as a consequence of the production process. It is generally accepted that a factory fault has no, or very little, effect on the perceived visual acceptance of a piece or indeed the price of a piece, (or so many people say). Quite frankly, if the defect is visible to the casual glance, it will have an effect, not only on how the viewer reacts to the piece but also the market price for the piece. If such a fault can only be found by looking underneath the piece or in fairly hidden place, such as the underside of a handle joint, then the defect becomes less significant and therefore less detrimental.

Restoration is a very different matter. The need for restoration implies a significant reduction in the value of a piece, no matter what you've been told or what the person selling the piece may try to say. There are some exceptions however but more of that later. There are two types of restoration, one known as 'museum' and the other generally called 'invisible', which is odd seeing as it rarely is, once the eye becomes tuned. The latter is so called, as it is out to try and deceive the viewer that the object is perfect. To be clear here, we are not talking about 'fakes', this is an entirely different field that we will deal with in another section.

Museum restoration, in terms of ceramics, is where an object is returned to how it would have looked, by the replacing of a hand, handle, piece of the rim, surface enamel, etc, thereby giving the viewer a more complete understanding of the piece. Such restoration is more often than not quite apparent, even to the uninitiated interested in such matters, and always intended to be reversible.

The invisible type of restoration, which is more commonly found, or should I say 'too commonly found', on the open market, is, more often than not, meant to make any unwary buyer part with more money than the object is worth. Here again, as with factory faults, the choice, if there is one, is entirely up to the buyer. There is nothing wrong with buying restored items, so long as you know they are restored, they are sold as such and the price reflects the amount of restoration the item has undergone. A few, very few, items can have a greater value because of the restoration, but these in the main are for those pieces which would otherwise have been in many pieces and rarity makes restoration essential to better understand and appreciate the object. At this stage I should say that in some rare instances, talking generally about the ceramics, antiques and the collectibles market, it has been known for the supposed, leaders in a certain field or type of ceramics to knowingly sell restored items that have not been labeled as such. It really is down to the buyer to make him or herself aware of the condition of an object and any restoration. As will be seen later on, this is a far easier task than you might think.

The perennial problem is that too often items are deliberately sold as perfect, when they are anything but, the condition of the object being either not mentioned or ignored. That is not to say, of course, that the person/institution selling the item is always aware that the item had been restored in the first place. You may well find that the vendor might well have bought the item, in good faith, as being perfect or only restored in a very small area. One of the GOLDEN RULES of buying is never assume anything until you have satisfied yourself of the condition of an item. In other words, to use that well-worn phrase "caveat emptor". That said, if you are actually looking to have a return, in terms of some sort of investment, out of your collecting, so that you can plough your funds into better, larger or rarer pieces later on, then buying restored items will generally not give you much return for your outlay. Speaking from experience, it is not very nice having to tell someone that many of the pieces that they have been buying for the last ten or fifteen years are worth less than half what they might have paid for them in good faith. If you wish to build up a study collection involving certain decorative techniques or types of body, then the condition of the pieces you buy might be of little consequence, price and diversity of objects being considerations that are more important.

So how do you spot restoration? What is restoration? Do you need any special tools to help discover restored items, such as ultraviolet lights? Are you likely to come across many restored items? Such questions rather depend on your level of collecting, meaning the amount of funds you put into your collection, where you buy your piece and such like. For example, if you buy from one or two specialist dealers then those dealers should be your eyes and ears, offering you advice and knowledge, as well as guarantees of authenticity. After all many such dealers thrive on the repeat business. If, on the other hand, you buy infrequently and mainly from various antique fairs and shops on your travels, then you need to be a great deal more discerning as to the condition of pieces, having to rely on your own judgement. The acquiring of such judgement may, at first, seem a little daunting; however, you will be surprised by how rapidly your skills at spotting restored pieces will grow.

For the purposes of this book, what follows is directly concerned with the wares made by at the Wileman/Shelley pottery, meaning wares made from earthenware and fine bone china.

Firstly I think it is necessary to say a few words about factory faults, as they are a relatively common occurrence amongst the wares of this pottery, but for good reason. The most common wares that you will find in this category are the high quality fine bone china tablewares of the 1890s through to 1920s, rather than the very earliest average quality wares of the 1860s and 1870s. There are several reasons for this but the main one, from which the others stem, is the body itself. The particular high quality body, which itself was refined still further with the introduction of the famous 'Dainty White' range in 1896, was unique to the pottery, later becoming synonymous with Shelley wares. The problem was that the materials used, or rather the proportions needed to produce such a brilliant and translucent wares made the body less malleable and more difficult to fire consistently well. In an effort to produce a certain high quality feel and look to the ware, problems occurred in consistent quality production. In terms of running a business, and in this both Joseph Shelley followed by his son Percy were extremely adept, such problems would have been resolved in numerous ways. Having different categories or standards of end product, sold to the markets that would tolerate such standards, would have been a typical solution, the very best wares often being sold in America, the seconds in Britain and the thirds to bulk purchasers for sale at the market level or to other foreign countries.

So what you will find, in terms of defects, are teacups, saucers, teapots, bowls, etc., with internal cracks in the body, often under the glaze, usually at the rim where the body is particularly thin, fractures where the handle joins, or should join, the body. You can find such blemishes by placing the objects in front of a powerful light try taking the shade off a table lamp with a 100 watt bulb and place the object near to the bulb (For best results place a hand between your eyes and the light bulb, so that you can see the object properly, at the same time preserving your eyesight.).

By looking at objects in this way you will also find other blemishes, such as what appear to be holes or eruptions in the glaze, usually the size of a pinhead. That is more or less what they are, having been caused by an air bubble trapped in the cold wet glaze, which due to the heat of the kiln explodes or bursts open. This last detail also reveals the mechanics of what causes the internal cracks, namely a stress in the body material, when thicker in one part than another, such as the base of a cup when compared to the rim, under the influence of heat. Basically when a ceramic object is fired the material shrinks, particularly bone china, so if there is a difference in thickness. It logically follows that the rate of shrinkage will be different. What you might also notice under the light are some irregular patches and also some black specks. The former is again due to an inconsistency in the body material which, as mentioned above, is not as malleable as is might be. The later is a foreign body or a bit of dust. Inevitable really.

Another blemish that seems not to have bothered to production line inspector was the shape of many of the pieces, particularly flat wares, such as saucers and plates, as well as cups and bowls. Turn many such pieces upside down and see the result. You will find, without much effort, that many of the pieces you try will have a distinct wobble or if you look directly at the opening of a cup or two many are far from circular!

Restoration says much about the object and potentially about the vendor. The only reasons for getting anything restored are because the piece is very rare, even unique; if you like the object enough to pay for cost of restoration, regardless of the value, if restoration gives the viewer a better understanding of the object or purely to deceive someone that the object is perfect. Whatever your position it is entirely personal.

The following, however, should help those that wish to know how to spot restoration, and in my experience 98% of restoration is discernible, by eye, meaning without resorting to major violence such as scraping the whole object with a pin or knife to remove the restoration. If you did this in front of someone's stand at an antique fair or in his or her shop, you would probably be liable for criminal damage. Anyway, such methods show a complete lack of professionalism, which only novice collectors/dealers or the uniformed can be seen doing. Lets face it, at four o'clock in the afternoon at a big antique fair the chances of discovering that perfect bargain are pretty slim, unless the trader has suddenly discovered a box under the table or the severe weather warnings and remoteness of the fair site kept all the dealers and collectors at home!

The most eminently restorable type of ware made by the Shelley pottery is the so-called Intarsio range. Why? Well, because the wares are made of earthenware and were decorated with blocks of bold colours in largish areas, as well as having the handles, rims and feet painted in on-glaze enamels. All of which makes for a restorer's dream. You will find a large quantity of this type of ware has been restored and often very well. Chips to the rims and feet are very difficult to detect, from the casual glance, as are re-glued or made up handles and finials. Difficult but by no means impossible to spot. How do you spot restoration? The first thing to understand is what restoration involves and what it comprises.

Restoration, at it's most basic, is plastic. Or put another way bone china and earthenware, for our purposes, have been fired up to temperatures in the region of 1400°C and 1000°C respectively and the restoration if fired at all, will only have been 'warmed' by comparison. The implication of this statement is that the fired ceramics will be very, very hard, indeed covered with a cold glass-like material called glaze. Restoration, on the other hand, will be soft and more often than not, warmer to the touch. The rest I think you can probably guess. You can spot restoration, particularly on glazed wares, by running your fingernail over the surface of the glaze of an item. On a perfectly normal piece your fingernail will move quickly across the hard, glass-like surface. You can even gently tap the surface of the pot and hear the high pitched tone, as well as feel the hardness of the surface. On a restored piece your fingernail will glide over the unaltered part of the surface then suddenly meet resistance on the softer restored part of the body. Tapping the restored area will produce a far duller tone than previously heard.

Another method of spotting restoration is to tap the rim, handle, hand, arm or whatever, with your teeth. All sounds rather unhygienic, but it is highly effective, if somewhat amusing to the onlooker. Once my suspicions had been raised, far from seemingly biting the object concerned, which was the usual retort, the hard enamel of your teeth, if only very gently tapped against an object, would provide more than enough evidence of a hard or tell-tail soft spot on a pot.

What is highly unprofessional and more of a sign of ignorance and laziness, is to get a coin out your pocket or a pin of some kind and start scraping it across the surface of a pot. The most obvious thing that will happen it that any restoration will immediately have a long and unsightly gouge left in it. The owner is likely to be somewhat upset if only after this event, do you think to look at the label where it mentions the restoration. In such a case the seller would be justified in asking for, at the very least, compensation for the damage to the restoration and possibly that you buy the object in question. I only mention this because it has been known to happen. In any case, using metal objects to reveal restoration is, as I mentioned, unprofessional, indicating that you don't really know what you're doing.

That is not the last of it by any means, as you can confirm your suspicions by feeling the temperature of a pot. In other words, restoration retains heat more than the glazed surface of a pot. You can try this by holding a suspect or known area of restoration in your palm, or in some form apply the heat from your hand onto the restored area, holding the rim, arm, handle, etc, for ten or fifteen seconds or so. Then, returning your hand, after a similar period of time, to the same part of the item, you will feel that the temperature has not altered greatly, compared to the glazed part of the item.

Once you become more accustomed to spotting restoration, your eyes immediately homing in on likely areas to have suffered damage or knocks. You will find that there are more subtle ways of finding restored areas such as slight variations in colour. Equally as noticeable are dull patches where they should reflect the light more strongly, which can be caused as much by the soft varnished surface over a restored area as by the irregularity of such a false surface. This is rather like spotting a re-sprayed area on the bodywork of a car, those distortions and funny irregular wavy-lines that you see when you catch the surface in the right light. Whatever you try and do and no matter how well it is done, the re-sprayed panels of a car are never quite going to have that original factory look. The same with a piece of ceramic.

At the end of the day one of the most important skills you will develop in this field is the ability to spot likely places where damage to an object might have occurred to warrant restoration. You can not do this successfully by just looking at the object from five feet away, you do need to pick the object up and handle it. If there is nothing else that you come away with after reading this section then at least file in the appropriate memory bank that you won't learn a thing unless you develop the confidence to handle objects, no matter what price they are. If you wish to pick up things with impunity then try the auction houses, after all the whole purpose for their existence is to act as an agent between vendor and purchaser and you are hardly going to purchase anything without inspecting it. Anyway, auction houses are insured and have friendly, trained staff in specialist departments that want to you to bid for what is on display.

One or two other types of restoration you might see, still talking about the two main types of ware used at the Shelley works, are the covering of surfaces scratches, the use of penciled imitation crazing and over painting or re-touching of surface enamel and/or gilt. As already mentioned above, the way of spotting such repair is to hold the item in your hands and actually study it. You need to be able to see the reflections on the glaze to help indicate the restored or masked areas, also the irregularities of the softer surface. Covering surface scratches is usually carried out by coating the whole surface of the piece, mostly plates, with a very fine film of imitation glaze, plastic spray, liquefied nail varnish or whatever. Then end result, once caught in the right light, inevitably leaves very faint trails or creases in the surface.

The use of pencilled lines can be found where the restored area needs to retain the look of remainder of the object, which might be glaze-crazed. The restorer simply pencils onto the restored area fake irregular crazed lines, before coating the area with the imitation glaze. The end result, on inspection, often reveals odd far from straight unconnected lines. You can imagine the effect by just drawing short irregular lines, some connecting some not, on a piece of paper.

Touching up the enamel is often difficult to spot because it is not something that one normally considers when assessing an object. For this you need a good eye for colour and tonal variations. In the worst cases whole areas or colours are removed from the surface of the glaze and replaced which, of course, solves the problem of trying to match a colour that might be seventy years old. If this is not done then it is easier to spot colour and tonal variations.

In the case of bone china, there is a tool that will be of great help, namely a torch. By torch, I'm thinking of a small body with a very powerful beam. In other words, a torch with a head that you could fit inside the narrow neck of a vase or up with the base of a figure, so that the figure, vase, cup or whatever, can act as a lamp shade. Through the use of a torch you will generally be able to spot any restored areas very easily, as they will be shown up as dark patches or lines that appear in an otherwise clear body. I say generally, as there will inevitably be some areas, such as a handle, arm, wrist, knop, where it will be impossible to get light through. Spotting repaired chips to the rim of plates, bowls and other such items can also be done with a torch.

The use of a torch comes in to it's own when you are looking for damage on bone china, especially hairline cracks. Fine hairline cracks are relatively common on the Shelley fine bone china body, as previously mentioned, because of the consistency of the material and the inherent firing problems. You will also be able to find fine stress cracks that appear in the clay body under the glaze, as well as other factory faults, such as lapparentight patches in the body where the walls have become very thin due to a lack of clay, more often than not caused by a badly cleaned mould.

Gilt is the last item to be applied to a piece of ceramics and is fired on at the lowest temperature. It is also the first to disappear through use, normally rubbing and/or scraping due to washing and general wear and tear. There are a few other ways gilt can disappear and one them is for someone to deliberately rub it off. Why would someone do this? Well, if someone has bought a complete tea/dinner/dessert service with no cracks or chips, but with many pieces having badly worn gilt then there might be a temptation to tidy everything up by taking off all the gilt and selling it as perfect. You can imagine the scenario whereby only two or four cups, saucers and side plates only ever get used out of a larger set, leaving a varied condition to the pieces. In some cases there may have been only a limited use of gilt on the pattern such that it wouldn't be obviously missing to the untrained eye. This is just another thing that given time you will learn to take into consideration when assessing something you are looking at, especially if you, like so many collectors, are buying trios or just one representative piece of a certain shape with as many patterns on it as you can find.

As a slight aside, for those in the know, the reason for "The Shelley Ping" or rather the occasions when it doesn't, is due to the variability in the viscosity or thickness of the glaze combined with the variable consistency of the body. During the early years of the twentieth century the mixing of both glaze and body materials was not an exact or 100% accurate science, which resulted in minor variable batches of glaze and body material. A more viscous glaze will produce a low toned note or ping than a similar piece with a thinner glaze. The minor fluctuation of the body has a similar effect. In more recent years, such variability has been processed out of much of the industry by the availability of ready made/mixed glazes and body material.

Fakes

This is not a chapter that I ever like to see in a book but unfortunately it is one that is necessary. Look at it in a positive way: There are those that say that when fakes start to appear then something must be worth money to warrant the fakes. For others this can be a rather off-putting aspect of the world of collecting.

Thankfully this is only a very short chapter, indicating that very little has been faked from the Shelley range. Hopefully, by keeping on top of the situation, through the collector's clubs and in other books such as this, then it might deter the fakers from starting to produce the ware in the first place.

Only recently, December 1998, whilst wondering around an antique establishment in Cambridgeshire I came across what can only be described as a very clever fake. Clever, I might add only because the plate and mark were original but the surface decoration was not. The item concerned was a dinner plate, 10 inches, with what looked to be a Mabel Lucie Attwell child, with typical exaggerated round head and puffed out checks, playing cricket. Having never seen this design on a Shelley plate I examined it more closely, only then were the tell-tail amateurish unskilled hands of the painter/paintress more noticeable. The colours began to seem slightly strange and off-putting, but more apparent was the lack of draughtsmanship. The plate itself was genuine with an original transfer printed factory mark, so it was either an original undecorated white glazed plate (possibly a seconds ware piece) or it had previously had a pattern that had been taken off. Hopefully this piece has now been put into the owners 'Black Museum' or perhaps one has now been started, being put down to the experience that goes with the job.

Another fake to report is of a figure. This fake was discussed in the December 1994 issue of the Shelley Group Newsletter, under the title 'Beware of the Dog'. The item in question is a fake of a model designed by Mabel Lucie Attwell in 1937 depicting an elf sitting astride a dog, on a grassy mound. The fake is some .5cm smaller than the original which is 7 cm high and the colours have a more pastel appearance. It would appear that the fake has an unusual coloured brown/black 'Shelley. England.' mark with an indistinct 'Fine Bone China' under the glaze.

Backstamps

Many pottery backstamps do not always tell the whole truth about an object, in terms of the exact year(s) of its use. In a commercial enterprise, whilst the trading name of a company may change and with its associated mark, or indeed just the mark, the use of new marks did not always start or the registered alteration. If a company had twenty or thirty thousand backstamps lying about unused it would hardly throw them away. In many instances items of a certain shape or pattern are known to have been introduced on a certain plate or month, yet appear with backstamps indicating an earlier date. An immediate example that springs to mind are the numerous Royal Albert wares that were produced James the Shelley factory after the takeover still made use of the Shelley backstamp. What follows therefore can only ever be a rough guide. There are also many variations of some of the marks below, some additional names of the type of Ware involved and/or pattern names.

James F. Wileman 1870 to 1892
Monochrome black or blue transfer-printed marks.

Wileman & Co 1872 to 1910
Monochrome transfer-printed marks in a variety of colours often in the same colour as the surface pattern.

Shelley China 1910 to 1966
Renamed "Shelley China Limited" in 1965, having registered the name 'Shelleys' as the company trade name in 1925.

ENGLAND

1912-1925
Late Foley' added
1910 to 1916

1925-1945
'Fine Bone China' added in
1945 and used until 1966

1930-1932
Also to be found on
Miniatures in the 1950s

Along the way other marks were used such as that used on the wares produced during the collaboration between 'Shelleys' and Gosling & Jackson. The mark, as has been mentioned earlier, consisted of the names "Shelley" and " Grosvenor China" with "and" in between and was produced using a black ink stamp.

   There is also the oval wreath and ribbon mark found on commemorative wares, dating from about 1936-37 and the name "Shelley China" in capitals together with a number used on heraldic wares.

SHELLEY CHINA
370

On the Internet . . .

This chapter speaks for itself, but would such a chapter have been included in a book a couple of years or even a year ago? Probably not. Even now the only reason for adding such a chapter would be because there was sufficient interest to do so. Well there is quite frankly plenty of interest to be found in Shelley China by surfing the Net. Some, indeed hopefully many of you, may even have found this very book via a search on the Net or perhaps as a consequence of it.

For those of you who have yet to browse the World Wide Web then I can say, "what is there on the Net for the Shelley collector?" To which the reply would be, "read on and you'll find out." For those of you already familiar with and have even perhaps 'book marked' the sites of interest related to Shelley then this might be old news, but you never know.

All you have to do is search for 'Shelley China' and away you go. Well almost. What you will find is that there are one or two other Shelley's, such as the poet, Percy B Shelley, who will crop up and get in the way. A more dedicated search specifying what to leave out might also help. You will also find that searching on 'Shelley Wileman', 'Shelley Pottery', 'Shelley Dainty' and such names will produce specific and interesting results.

At the time of writing there are some 30 sites related to Shelley, when you search as above, but this is a tiny fraction as these sites come from one search engine. Even now there are still various ways of finding out information about Shelley, for example current or recent prices, by searching the various auction house sites or, even better, do a specific search on 'Artfact' which is a compilation of numerous auction house catalogues. There are various other sites such as Thesaurus.

One of the most interesting looking web sites is the 'Shelley China Mailing List' which appears to have been going for about two years. This is certainly a good place to start for the new Shelley surfer as it offers details about Shelley groups & clubs, published books, illustrations of shapes with their names, details, etc, a wants list, bargains and most importantly other 'links'. The Shelley China Mailing List is just that a free list of like minded collectors and dealers, who can keep in touch with the latest world wide news, offers, wants lists, new clubs that might develop, etc, even new books. To find out more about this list you can try the above, namely search under Shelley China or you can contact:- jmason@island.net

I think this perhasp goes without saying but I will say it anyway. There are basically two types of service available on the internet, those sites, namely the Clubs and Societies, who are dedicated to providing information about the wares, history of the pottery, types of shape & pattern, different types of wares, marks, etc and those sites where you can find out where to buy and sell Shelley wares, along with related sites where you can find out prices.

Another site of interest for those seeking specific pieces in certain patterns and shapes is the antiques connection – www.antiqueconnectiuon.com. Here you are given tick boxes to fill in indicating the pattern (34 in all with an option to add others), edge colours, shapes (only 6 to choose from plus option) and the type of piece you want from a choice of 21 with an option to add others. Having filled in the form you hit send and should expect to hear within three weeks. This type of 'china matching' service is something that has been growing in popularity in the UK and USA.

I have listed the Shelley Groups and Clubs that I can find on a separate page. What is interesting to note is that two of the groups/clubs have researchers based in the UK that will find out anything you want to know about the wares you have from the Shelley archive, which is owned by the Royal Doulton factory. Having spent many hours in the archive myself I can quite honesty say that the vast majority of questions you might have, related to the archive, you will be able to find the answers in the books mentioned in the bibliography. I say this because the three books – *Wileman* by Richard Knight and Susan Hill, *The Shelley Style* by Susan Hill and *Shelley Pottery – The Later Years* by Chris Davenport, all have lists or indexes of a great many of the patterns and shapes extracted directly from the remaining pattern books.

Don't forget, even if you find exactly what you are looking for, that vital last piece of the set, that the costs of shipping the item may be twice the price, or more, of the piece itself. The only other thing to be sure about is that you are perfectly aware of and happy about the condition of the piece you are getting. Ask for a receipt/letter/fax or even an email that specifically covers the condition of the piece you are interested in as well as arrangements for returning something that is not in the condition/colour/shape you thought or agreed that it would be. I say 'shape' because, as I have indicated in the 'Restoration and Abnormalities' chapter, cup/teapot/any handles can be off-centre, shapes can also be distorted in the firing, lids can be matched, etc. Why not create your own tick box list making a summary features for the person selling the item to fill in and return/fax/email to you?

Buying from dealers/collectors should be no different from buying through a reputable auction house, the ones with the guarantees that specify that if the items are not as specified/viewed/reported on that you can return them to the auction house. This is why it might be advisable to create your own set of criteria/conditions of business that require a signature or response before embarking on any transaction. It might prevent some problems later.

Shelley Groups & Clubs

U.K. Shelley Group
Formed in 1986 this group has a wide international as well as national following. There are four colour magazines a year, together with news of two specialist Shelley fairs that are organised each year. There are regional social gathering are organised for members to meet up and talk about each others collections and latest finds as well as access to the Shelley Pattern books and archive but only through club research officers.

Membership costs – single £15.00, dual £20.00. Overseas – single £20.00, dual £25.00. You can also pay in US Dollars. If you wish to join you can either e-mail stephen@hugher.demon.co.uk or write, with your postal address, to: Linda Ellis (treasurer), 228 Croyland Road, Lower Edmonton, London, N9 7BG, England. UK.

Australian Shelley Club
Established in 1983 this appears to be the oldest club and has a worldwide membership who receive four newsletters a year, in which members are able to advertise for free. Cost for membership is AUS$20 per year within Australia, whether single or dual. For more information contact: – Greg Hammond at greghmnd@nrg.com.au

National Shelley China Club
This club was formed in 1990 and has an international membership of over 500 dedicated to learning and disseminating knowledge concerning all aspects of Shelley wares. New members receive a packet of nine pages of material about Shelley books, publications, the club and its officers as well as security and events. When joining you will also get all the previous newsletters in the same year. For your membership you get, amongst other things, a quarterly twenty-four page, or thereabouts, newsletter with at least two pages of colour.

The club also sponsors a National Conference and at least one "All-Shelley" Show. The conference for 1999 is to be in Atlanta, Gerogia, for three days from 13th June. The first planned Show is on 13 March 1999 at Maitland, Florida.

Membership costs – $35 for a new member ($40 if non-US), with renewals on 1st January of $25 thereafter. For more information and an application, write to: Curt Leiser. 12010 38th Ave. NE Seattle., WA 98125 or E-mail Curt Leiser at cleiser@compuserve.com

New Zealand Shelley Collectors Group
The NZ Shelley Collectors Group is a small group of Shelley (and other marks) collectors mostly living in the Auckland area. They meet about 4 times a year at a member's home and talk about what they have seen and bought. More information is available on the group by contacting June Hearne, their newsletter editor, at june.hearne@adis.co.nz or by writing to The Shelley Collectors Club. Glenys Ryall, 9 Fowey Avenue, Te Atatu South, Auckland.

If nothing else it will be worthwhile keeping in touch with these clubs, via e-mails or letter, just to find out when there might be a specific Shelley fair or conference. Two such events happen regularly, although the venue might change. During March there is usually a Shelley Show in Florida which is billed as the world's largest all Shelley show. In June there is usually a Shelley conference. Details of these annual events are distributed through some of the clubs and societies but also on the Internet.

Bibliography

Books
Shelley Potteries: The History & Production of a Staffordshire Family of Potters *Chris Watkins, William Harvey & Robert Senft* Barrie & Jenkins. 1986.
Wileman *Richard Knight & Susan Hill* Jazz Publications. 1995.
The Shelley Style – A Collectors Guide *Susan Hill* Jazz Publications. 1990.
Shelley Pottery – The later years *Chris Davenport* Chris Davenport and Heather Productions Ltd. 1997.
Twentieth Century Design – Ceramics *Frances Hannah* Bell & Hyman. 1986.
20th Century Ceramics *Gordon Forsyth* The Studio Publications. 1936.
Encyclopaedia of British Art Pottery *Victoria Bergesen* Barrie & Jenkins. 1991.
Design in British Industry *Michael Farr* University Press, Cambridge. 1955.
Twentieth-Century Design *Jonathan M Woodham* Oxford University Press. 1997.
Midwinter– A Collectors' Guide *Alan Peat* Cameron & Hollis. 1992.

Journals
Pottery Gazette & Glass Trades Review
Pottery Gazette & Glass Trades Review – Directory & Diary
Pottery & Glass Record
The Studio magazine
The Studio Decorative Art Year Book (various years)
The Art Journal
Design

Catalogues/Newsletters
The Shelley Pattern Books, Courtesy of Royal Doulton (UK) Ltd.
The Shelley Standard magazine
Shelley Retail catalogues, four in all produced in the 1930s
Shelley Pottery – 1774-1966 Travelling exhibition Catalogue the Geffrye Museum, London. 1980.
The Shelley Group Newsletter
Thirties – British Art and Design before the war Hayward Gallery Exhibition catalogue. 1979.

Auction catalogues, Sotheby's, Christie's South Kensington, Louis Taylor (Hanley),Bonhams.

Others
Interviews with two former Shelley workers.
Various Web Sites

BEVERLEY

London's leading specialist of Shelley and Wileman

Visit our shop with its extensive range of English and European Art Deco pottery

Monday–Thursday – 11.00am–6.00pm

Friday and Saturday – 9.30am–6.00pm

Sundays – By appointment

**30 Church Street
Marylebone, London NW8 8EP
Tel/Fax: 020 7262 1576
Mobile 0467 783956**

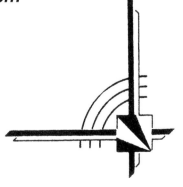

Robert Prescott-Walker MA (Dip)

Specialist Decorative Arts Consultant 1851-Present

Author, Lecturer and Appraiser.

Expert advice given on all aspects of developing a collection or period interior styling. All aspects of the decorative arts from the 1850s to the present. Available for professional guidance on matters of authenticity, originality and condition concerning objects.
22 years knowledge in the field and 14 years experience working with and in the antiques and auction business.

Individual and/or group tuition given on:
Buying & Selling
Auction/trade/fairs/private/Internet

How to look at an object
Shape/surface pattern/materials/restoration
Decorative Arts history

For further information and enquiries,
write to the publisher,
Francis Joseph Publications
5 Southbrook Mews, London. SE12 8LG UK
or Email at:
chrisandrob@earthlink.net

Notes